OSLO TRAVEL GUIDE 2024

Your Essential Travel Companion to Explore Norway's
Vibrant Capital - Top Must-See Attractions, History,
Culture, Adventure And Unique Experiences.

Nicholas Ingram

Oslo Opera House

Tjuvholmen

Aker Brygge

Tøyen Bibliotek

El Pez Oslo

Bygdøy dusk

She Lies

Bjørvika Barcode

The Acrobat Bridge

The Royal Palace

Vigeland Park fountain

The Munch Museum

Holmenkollen Ski Jump

Norwegian Museum of Cultural History

Karl Johans gate at night

The Nobel Peace Center

The Kon-Tiki Museum

DISLCAIMER & COPYRIGHT NOTE

Disclaimer

The information in this guide is based on the author's experiences, research, and knowledge up to the publication date. While efforts have been made to ensure accuracy, the author and publisher are not liable for changes, inaccuracies, or omissions after this date. Travel conditions may change, and readers should independently verify details before making arrangements. The author and publisher do not assume responsibility for readers' actions following the guide, as travel involves inherent risks. Readers are advised to exercise caution and make informed decisions based on their individual circumstances.

Copyright Note

CONTENTS

About this Guide 1

CHAPTER 1: INTRODUCTION 3

Welcome to Oslo 4

Why Visit Oslo 6

A Brief History of Oslo 10

CHAPTER 2: PLANNING YOUR TRIP 13

Visas, Currency & Exchange 15

Packing Essentials 17

Getting to Oslo 19

Getting Around Oslo 20

CHAPTER 3: EXPLORE OSLO TOP CHOICES ... 22

Must-See Sights 23

Museums 32

Parks 46

Neighborhoods 53

Walking Oslo 59

Hiking Oslo 63

Tours 67

Oslo Unique Experiences 69

Other Attractions Worth Seeing in Oslo 73

CHAPTER 4: WHERE TO STAY IN OSLO 75

Best Budget Friendly Accomodation to Stay in Oslo ... 77

Best Mid-Range Accomodation to Stay in Oslo ... 80

Best Luxurious Accomodation to Stay in Oslo ... 83

CHAPTER 5: SAVORING NORWEGIAN CUISINE ... 86

What to Eat in Oslo 87

Restaurants & Must-Try Dishes   90

Cooking Classes   95

Street Food Spots   97

CHAPTER 6: OSLO FESTIVAL AND NIGHTLIFE THRILL   98

Oslo Festival   99

Must-Witness Annual Festivals   100

Oslo Nightlife   102

Top Choice Nightlife Venues   103

CHAPTER 7: BEYOND OSLO - DAY TRIPS & NEARBY ADVENTURES   105

Top 10 Day Trips & Excursions from oslo   106

Day trips by car: Art, crafts and industrial history   113

Green Day Trips in the Oslo Region With Bus and Trains   115

A Day Trip By The Waters   117

CHAPTER 8: OSLO ON A BUDGET   121

Budgeting Advice   122

Free Attractions in Oslo   124

Less than $20 Dining Venues in Oslo   125

Affordable Places to Stay in Oslo   127

Budget-Friendly Sightseeing Options in Oslo   128

Explore Oslo's Art Scene on a Budget   129

Explore Free Parks & Outdoor Attractions   131

Explore Free Events in Oslo   133

Oslo Pass   134

CHAPTER 9: ESSENTIAL INFORMATION & TIPS   135

Communication Tips   136

50 Useful Norwegian phrases to Navigate Your Way in Oslo   137

Staying Safe & Healthy   142

Accessibility & Family Travel   144

Sustainable Travel: Making Eco-Friendly Choices in Oslo   146

Shopping & Souvenirs   148

CHAPTER 10: THEMED ITINERARIES   150

Art Aficionado   151

Gastronome Explorer   153

Adventure Enthusiast   155

History Enthusiast   157

 BONUS CHAPTER   158

Hidden Gems & Off-the-Beaten-Path Adventures   159

Seasonal Highlights   161

Oslo 2024 Festival Calendar   164

What to Read And Watch Before Visiting Oslo   166

Useful Websites   168

Recommended Apps   169

Say Goodbye & Take a Piece of Norway with You   171

ABOUT THIS GUIDE

Welcome to the ultimate travel guide to Oslo, your comprehensive companion for an unforgettable journey through the vibrant capital of Norway. Whether you're a culture enthusiast, a nature lover, or a gastronomic explorer, this guide is crafted to cater to every traveler's interests and preferences. Inside this guide, you will get information about:

1. Thorough Planning Assistance: Dive into Chapter 2 for essential information on visas, currency, packing tips, and navigating your way to and around Oslo.

2. Exploring Oslo's Wonders: Chapter 3 unfolds the city's treasures, guiding you through must-see sights, museums, parks, and unique experiences that define Oslo's charm.

3. Accommodation Choices: Discover the perfect place to stay with insights into budget-friendly, mid-range, and luxurious accommodations in Chapter 4.

4. Savoring Norwegian Cuisine: Chapter 5 takes you on a culinary journey, highlighting what to eat, must-try dishes, cooking classes, and the best street food spots in Oslo.

5. Festival and Nightlife Thrills: Immerse yourself in Oslo's vibrant festival scene and nightlife options in Chapter 6, ensuring your evenings are as lively as your days.

6. Day Trips & Adventures Beyond Oslo: Chapter 7 introduces you to exciting day trips and nearby adventures, providing options for every traveler's interest.

7. Oslo on a Budget: Chapter 8 caters to budget-conscious travelers with advice on free attractions, affordable dining, and wallet-friendly accommodations.

8. Essential Information & Tips: Chapter 9 offers valuable insights, including communication tips, useful Norwegian phrases, safety guidelines, and sustainable travel choices.

9. Themed Itineraries: Chapter 10 tailors itineraries for various interests, from art and gastronomy to exploration and adventure.

10. Bonus Chapter: Uncover hidden gems, off-the-beaten-path adventures, seasonal highlights, the Oslo 2024 Festival Calendar, and recommendations for your pre-travel reading and viewing.

Embark on your Oslo adventure armed with the knowledge and recommendations that will make your trip truly exceptional. Say goodbye to Oslo, but take a piece of Norway with you using the insights from this guide. Happy travels!

CHAPTER 1: INTRODUCTION

WELCOME TO OSLO

Ahoy there, Welcome to Oslo, where Viking whispers brush against fjord-kissed skyscrapers, and history intertwines with hyper-cool happenings like a Viking braid woven with neon thread. Get ready to dive into a city that's equal parts rugged explorer and sophisticated charmer, where culture pops brighter than the aurora borealis and nature steals your breath like a perfectly timed ski jump.

Imagine this: you stroll through cobbled streets, echoing with tales of fearless Norsemen, before stumbling upon a sleek museum, its walls vibrating with contemporary art. You dine on fresh-caught fish from the fjord, washed down with craft beer brewed alongside Viking runes. Then, you dance the night away in a trendy club bathed in midnight sun, leaving the world spinning like a dizzying Holmenkollen descent.

But Oslo isn't just about contrasts, it's about connections. Hike through lush forests that hug the city, and suddenly you're a Viking trekking through ancient sagas. Kayak across the glassy fjord, and the water whispers stories of seafaring heroes. Explore Vigeland Park, where fantastical sculptures erupt from the earth, and you'll swear you've stumbled into a modern-day fairytale.

This city breathes art. Wander through Munch's tortured landscapes, then get lost in Astrup Fearnley's vibrant contemporary collection. Catch a concert in the Opera House, its glass roof mimicking the fjord's shimmering scales, or let the National Theatre transport you to the heart of Norwegian drama. Don't forget to check out street art hidden in unexpected corners, where colorful murals weave vibrant tales onto everyday brick.

Foodies, brace yourselves! Oslo's culinary scene is a melting pot of flavors, from traditional fish stews simmered in cast iron to Michelin-starred creations pushing the boundaries of taste. Dive into bustling food halls, each stall a portal to a different culinary adventure. Or savor the catch of the day at a harborside bistro, gulls swooping overhead as you clink glasses with a toast to good times.

And when the city lights dim, Oslo's nightlife ignites. From cozy jazz bars nestled in historic cellars to pulsating nightclubs echoing with the latest beats, there's a rhythm for every soul. Catch a midnight movie under the open sky, or join a bonfire bash at the beach, laughing with locals as the sun dips below the horizon. Oslo is a city that whispers secrets in the wind, invites you to chase adventures hidden in every corner, and welcomes you with a warm hygge hug.

WHY VISIT OSLO

1. Nature and Fjord Finesse: Oslo isn't just a city, it's a gateway to breathtaking natural beauty. Imagine kayaking through glassy fjords, their waters reflecting the snow-capped peaks like giant emeralds. Hike through lush forests that hug the city limits, feeling like a modern-day Viking trekking through ancient sagas. Take a ferry to Hovedøya island, where wild sheep roam amidst Viking ruins, whispering tales of the past. And let's not forget the Oslo Opera House, its shimmering titanium roof mimicking the fjord's ever-changing hues – architecture meets nature in a breathtaking tango.

2. Artistic Soul with a Viking Heart: Oslo thrums with a creative pulse that's impossible to ignore. Wander through Munch's tortured landscapes, then get lost in Astrup Fearnley's vibrant contemporary collection. Catch a concert in the Opera House, its glass roof mimicking the fjord's shimmering scales, or let the National Theatre transport you to the heart of Norwegian drama. Don't forget to check out street art hidden in unexpected corners, where colorful murals weave vibrant tales onto everyday brick. And for a truly unique experience, visit Vigeland Park, where fantastical sculptures erupt from the earth, each one a whimsical story frozen in stone.

3. Foodie Paradise with a Twist: Oslo's culinary scene is a melting pot of flavors, from traditional fish stews simmered in cast iron to Michelin-starred creations pushing the boundaries of taste. Dive into bustling food halls, each stall a portal to a different culinary adventure. Savor the catch of the day at a harborside bistro, gulls swooping overhead as you clink glasses with a toast to good times. Or grab a hot dog from a charming "pølsebod" – Oslo's street food icon – and join the locals for a taste of pure city life.

4. Nightlife that Never Sleeps: When the city lights dim, Oslo's nightlife ignites. From cozy jazz bars nestled in historic cellars to pulsating nightclubs echoing with the latest beats, there's a rhythm for every soul. Catch a midnight movie under the open sky, or join a bonfire bash at the beach, laughing with locals as the sun dips below the horizon. And for a truly local experience, check out a "syttende mai" celebration – Norway's Constitution Day – and experience the infectious joy that spills onto the streets.

5. Local Insights for Adventurers: Beyond the must-sees, Oslo hides secret gems waiting to be discovered. Rent a bike and explore the city's network of trails, stopping at hidden sculptures and charming cafes along the way. Take a ferry to Bygdøy, a peninsula dotted with museums like the Viking Ship Museum and the Kon-Tiki, where adventure whispers from every mast. And for a truly unique experience, try your hand at ice skating on the frozen Frogner Stadium, feeling like a champion athlete under the twinkling city lights.

Oslo is a city that whispers secrets in the wind, invites you to chase adventures hidden in every corner, and welcomes you with a warm Nordic hug. So come, let your inner Viking loose, soak up the artistic energy, and savor the taste of a city that's as vibrant as a sunset over the fjord. Oslo awaits, ready to write your own unforgettable chapter in its story.

Remember, this is just a starting point. Oslo is a city that thrives on exploration, so be ready to wander, get lost, and discover your own unique experiences. Bon voyage!

A BRIEF HISTORY OF OSLO

Oslo's history commenced circa 1000 AD, nestled by the captivating Oslofjord. Viking leader Harald Hardrada founded this city as a bustling trading hub, christening it "Ánslo." By 1130, it ascended to the status of Norway's capital, firmly establishing itself as a pivotal political and cultural nucleus.

Flourishing Amidst the Middle Ages and Religious Influence: The Middle Ages ushered in Oslo's prosperity. Akershus Fortress, erected in the 13th century, emerged as a critical bastion of defense. Religion held sway, evidenced by the construction of Oslo Cathedral in the 12th century and the inception of monasteries that significantly contributed to the realms of art, learning, and craftsmanship.

The Hanseatic League and the Impact of the Black Death: The 14th century witnessed the arrival of the formidable Hanseatic League, a coalition of German merchants, altering Oslo's landscape through trade dominance and the introduction of fresh architectural styles. However, the catastrophic onslaught of the Black Death in 1349 inflicted severe devastation, crippling population numbers and stalling developmental strides.

Renaissance Rejuvenation and the Danish Union: The 16th century sparked a cultural renaissance. King Christian IV of Denmark seized the chance to reconstruct Oslo post a 1624 conflagration, rechristening it as Kristiania. Danish cultural influence permeated architectural designs, linguistic shifts, and administrative frameworks.

Norwegian Independence and Emergence of National Identity: The 19th century marked a turning point. In 1814, Norway secured autonomy from Denmark, igniting a robust sense of national pride. The Romanticist movement flourished, extolling Norway's natural beauty and Viking heritage, reflected vividly in artistic expressions and literary works.

Industrial Revolution and Urban Expansion: The late 19th century Industrial Revolution metamorphosed Oslo into a bustling industrial hub. Shipyards, factories, and ports fostered economic prosperity while birthing societal challenges like poverty and inequality, propelling the rise of labor movements and political activism.

World Wars and the Era of Modernism: Oslo bore the brunt of Nazi Germany's occupation during World War II, etching a painful memory in its chronicles. Post-war optimism and modernity swept through the city. Architects such as Arne Korsmo spearheaded a functionalist movement, giving rise to landmarks like the Oslo City Hall, fundamentally shaping the city's contemporary visage.

Cultural Flourishing and Global Acknowledgment: The latter part of the 20th century and early 21st century cemented Oslo's status as a cultural powerhouse. The National Museum, Munch Museum, and Astrup Fearnley Museum showcased artistic prowess, while contemporary architectural marvels like the Oslo Opera House garnered worldwide acclaim.

Environmental Focus and a Sustainable Tomorrow: Recent years witnessed Oslo embracing its coastal locale and assuming a pioneering role in environmental sustainability. Fjord City, a transformative waterfront project, stands as a testament to this commitment. Oslo endeavors to achieve carbon neutrality by 2030, epitomizing its forward-thinking ethos.

A Tapestry of History and Culture: Oslo's past and present intricately entwine. Whispers of the Viking era reverberate through historical landmarks, while the Hanseatic League's architectural influence endures. Danish cultural imprints persist, yet Norwegian independence and national identity thrive. Oslo's embrace of modernity and sustainability paints a promising future for this vibrant cultural mosaic nestled by the fjord.

CHAPTER 2: PLANNING YOUR TRIP

Summer Bliss (June to August)
Weather: Warmest days, long daylight hours, and a vibrant city buzz. | *Crowds:* Expect peak season with higher prices and bustling attractions. | *Activities:* Kayak on the fjord, picnic in parks, soak up the midnight sun, enjoy outdoor concerts and festivals like the Øya Festival. | **Unique experiences:** Hike to Holmenkollen for stunning views, catch a performance at the National Theatre, join the Midsummer bonfire celebrations.

Autumnal Charm (September to November)
Weather: Crisp air, fewer crowds, and beautiful fall foliage. | *Activities:* Explore museums, indulge in cozy cafes, wander charming neighborhoods, and witness the Northern Lights (September-October). | **Unique experiences:** Attend the Oslo Food Festival, visit Akershus Castle for spooky Halloween events, enjoy the serene atmosphere of Bygdøy island.

Winter Wonderland (December to February)
Weather: Snowy landscapes, magical Christmas markets, and cozy winter atmosphere. | *Activities:* Ski down Holmenkollen, go ice skating at Frogner Stadium, sip hot chocolate by the fjord, and experience the festive cheer.

| **Unique experiences:** Attend the Lucia procession, participate in winter sports like ice hockey, enjoy traditional Christmas feasts with locals.

Spring Awakening (March to May)

Weather: Blossoming flowers, milder temperatures, and a sense of renewal.

| **Activities:** Hike through rejuvenated forests, picnic on sunny waterfront spots, explore art galleries, and enjoy the Kon-Tiki Museum on Bygdøy. |

Unique experiences: Celebrate Constitution Day (May 17th) with vibrant parades and festivities, witness the world-famous Holmenkollen Ski Festival, discover hidden gem museums like the Stenersen Museum.

Bonus Tip

Consider checking Oslo's annual event calendar before booking your trip to catch specific festivals, concerts, or sporting events that pique your interest.

No matter the season, Oslo offers something special. Choose the time that best suits your travel style and prepare to be enchanted by this vibrant city. Bon voyage!

VISAS, CURRENCY & EXCHANGE

Preparing for your Oslo escapade involves more than just packing swimsuits and hiking boots. Navigating visa requirements and currency logistics is equally crucial. So, let's equip ourselves with these essential details using our metaphorical compass:

Visa: The good news is that visitors from *North America*, *Europe*, *Australia*, and *New Zealand* generally enjoy visa-free access to Norway for stays up to 90 days within a 180-day period. All you need is your passport to set the stage for your adventures!

However, if you hail from a different country or plan an extended stay, it's advisable to consult the official Norwegian Immigration Service website at *https://www.udi.no/en* for comprehensive insights into visa prerequisites and application processes.

Currency: Oslo and Norway operate using the Norwegian Krone (NOK). While cash remains relevant for smaller purchases, credit cards are widely embraced.

Exchange Rates: Current exchange rate (as of January 10, 2024): 1 USD = 10.32 NOK. Check the current exchange rate here: *https://www.forbes.com/advisor/money-transfer/currency-converter/nok-usd* or *https://www.currencytransfer.com/currencies/transfer-nok-to-usd*

Exchange Recommendations: Consider withdrawing local currency from ATMs upon arrival for minor expenses. | Be mindful of potential withdrawal fees from banks; it's prudent to investigate your bank's policies and compare ATM charges prior to your journey.

Although exchanging foreign currency before departure from your home country is an option, scrutinize rates diligently and steer clear of airport kiosks notorious for steep markups.

In Norway, tipping isn't customary, so you need not factor that into your exchange calculations.

Payment Methods: Credit cards: Visa, Mastercard, and American Express find wide acceptance across Oslo.

Debit cards: Your debit card might function at ATMs and point-of-sale terminals, but confirm with your bank beforehand regarding potential fees or limitations.

Mobile payment systems: Apple Pay and Google Pay are gaining traction in Norway and can be utilized at select contactless terminals.

Additional Suggestions: Prior to your departure, consider downloading a currency converter app for convenient on-the-go conversions. | Explore the possibility of acquiring travel insurance that covers medical emergencies and trip cancellations. | Notify your bank about your travel plans to prevent triggering suspicious activity alerts on your card.

Armed with accurate information and logistical readiness, you can immerse yourself in the enchantment of Oslo sans any financial hitches.

PACKING ESSENTIALS

Before embarking on your oslo journey, let's ensure your luggage isn't just filled with essentials but holds the magical ingredients for an unforgettable adventure. So, grab your travel compass, and let's curate the ideal packing list for Oslo:

LAYERING ESSENTIALS

Insulating Base Layers: Consider Merino wool or synthetic thermals for layering beneath sweaters and jackets, particularly during spring and fall. | *Adaptable Mid-Layers:* Pack sweaters, fleeces, or lightweight jackets that can be mixed and matched based on weather conditions. | *Waterproof Attire:* Oslo's weather can be erratic, making a dependable waterproof ensemble vital. Look for breathable materials like Gore-Tex. | *Comfortable Footwear:* With extensive exploration ahead, prioritize comfortable shoes with good traction. Opting for hiking boots is ideal for more adventurous outings.

BLEND INTO THE CULTURE

Urban Fashion: Choose attire suitable for museum visits and dining out. Think of comfortable jeans, smart casual dresses, or chinos paired with blouses. | *Relaxation Attire:* Include comfortable clothing for unwinding in your accommodations or enjoying evening picnics. Consider packing joggers, leggings, and cozy sweaters. | *Swimwear (Optional):* If you plan on taking a plunge in the fjord or visiting a sauna, bring along your swimsuit and a quick-drying towel.

TAILORING FOR THE DESTINATION

Travel Adapter: Norway uses Type F plugs, so make sure to pack an adapter to keep your devices charged. | *Sun Protection:* Despite the season, the sun can be intense, particularly around water bodies. Pack sunscreen, sunglasses, and a hat. | *Reusable Water Container:* Oslo boasts safe drinking water, making a reusable bottle an eco-friendly choice that also saves money. | *Daypack:* A lightweight backpack comes in handy for carrying essentials while exploring the city or venturing into nature.

ENSURING SAFETY

Basic First-Aid Kit: Equip yourself with essentials like bandages, pain relievers, and allergy medications. | ***Travel Insurance:*** It's wise to have coverage for unforeseen medical expenses or travel disruptions. | ***Copies of Vital Documents:*** Create duplicates of your passport, ID, and travel insurance papers in case of misplacement. | ***Offline Maps:*** Utilize apps like Google Maps offline to navigate even without internet connectivity.

AMPLIFYING EXPERIENCES

Guidebook or Travel App: Taking a Physical copy of this guide with you will surely be very helpful in providing insights into Oslo's history, culture, and hidden treasures. | ***Language Assistance Tools:*** Learning a few basic Norwegian phrases can facilitate connections with locals. The section inside this guidebook on Useful Norwegian Phrases to navigate your way in Oslo will be very helpful here. | ***Camera and Portable Charger:*** Capture Oslo's charm and ensure your battery preserves your memories. | ***Journal or Notebook:*** Document your experiences, musings, and reflections to craft a personalized Oslo narrative. | ***Extra Tip:*** Consider including a compact *umbrella*, a *headlamp* for nighttime exploration, and a *universal adapter* for charging devices like laptops and cameras.

Wise packing isn't just about attire—it's about packing experiences. Select items that fuel your curiosity, to embrace Oslo's diverse offerings & craft a journey that lingers longer in your memory.

GETTING TO OSLO

BY AIR

**Direct Flights:** The quickest and most convenient option is to fly directly into Oslo Airport Gardermoen (OSL), Norway's main hub. Flights are available from most major cities globally, with approximate costs varying depending on season and origin. Consider budget airlines like Norwegian Air or Ryanair for deals.

**Indirect Flights:** Depending on your location, a connecting flight via major European hubs like Amsterdam or Stockholm might offer cheaper options. This can be a good choice if you have time and want to break up the journey.

BY SEA

**BY FERRY:** For a truly Viking-inspired experience, consider sailing to Oslo from Copenhagen or Kiel. DFDS Seaways offer comfortable ferry cruises with onboard amenities like restaurants, bars, and cabins, transforming the journey into a mini-vacation. Expect travel times around 18-24 hours and costs starting from around €150.

BY TRAIN

**Intercity Trains:** From Stockholm, Gothenburg, and Copenhagen, intercity trains offer a scenic and comfortable journey to Oslo. Travel times range from 4-8 hours, with approximate costs starting from €50. Consider booking in advance for better deals.

BY ROAD

**Car Rental:** If you plan on exploring beyond Oslo, renting a car can offer flexibility and independence. Expect costs to vary depending on the rental company and vehicle type. Be aware of potential toll roads and parking fees.

GETTING AROUND OSLO

T-bane (Metro): Oslo's efficient metro system whisks you through the city with six lines and stations dotted across the map. Single Adult tickets start at around 40 NOK, or opt for adult 24hour pass for unlimited travel (121 NOK). See tickt price list: *https://ruter.no/en*

Trams and Buses: These colorful networks cover wider areas than the metro, making them your go-to for exploring neighborhoods and landmarks. Tickets and passes work identically to the metro.

Ferries: A quintessential Oslo experience! Hop on a ferry to Bygdøy for museums and beaches, or take a fjord cruise for panoramic views. Single ferry tickets start at around 50 NOK.

Taxis: Plentiful and readily available, taxis offer convenience but come with a premium price. Expect fares to start around 100 NOK and increase with distance.

Car Rentals: If venturing beyond the city center, consider renting a car. Be aware of steep parking fees and potential toll roads.

Bikes: Oslo is a cyclist's paradise! Rent a bike from numerous stations and enjoy the city's extensive network of bike paths. Rates start at around 50 NOK per day.

Ekebergbanen Funicular: This charming red funicular railway takes you from the harbor to Ekebergparken, offering breathtaking views of the city and fjord.

Frognersetern Tram: Catch the iconic "Holmenkollbanen" tram, one of the world's steepest inclined railways, for a thrilling ride to the Holmenkollen ski jump.

Download apps: Use the *RuterReise app* for live public transport information and trip planning, or the *Citymapper app* for combined public transport and walking directions.

Validate tickets: Remember to validate your public transport tickets on the yellow machines before boarding.

Oslo Pass: Save on transportation, attractions, and museums with the Oslo Pass. Choose the duration that suits your trip.

Must-See Spots: Explore the Viking Ship Museum, marvel at the Holmenkollen ski jump, soak in the art at the National Gallery, wander the vibrant Akerselva river district, and lose yourself in the vast Vigeland Park sculptures.

CHALLENGES & CONSIDERATIONS

Limited late-night transport: Public transport operates until around 1:00 AM, but options diminish late at night.

Accessibility: While generally accessible, some older tram stations and historical buildings might pose challenges for people with mobility limitations.

Tickets: Make sure you have the correct ticket before boarding public transport. Fines for fare evasion are hefty.

Navigating Oslo is about blending efficiency with adventure. So,
mix and match your transport options, embrace the unexpected,
and let the city's rhythm guide your exploration.

CHAPTER 3: EXPLORE OSLO TOP CHOICES

(2)

MUST-SEE SIGHTS

Karl Johans gate is Oslo's main street, running from the Oslo Central Station (Oslo S) in the west to the Royal Palace in the east.

Reason to Explore it: It is worth exploring for its vibrant city life, day and night, featuring shops, restaurants, cafés, street musicians, and cultural landmarks like the National Theatre and the Stortinget.

Getting there: You can easily reach Karl Johans gate by starting at the Oslo Central Station (Oslo S), which is the western end of the street.

What to do there: When you get to Karl Johans gate, you can enjoy a leisurely stroll along the cobblestoned pedestrian section, explore shops and eateries, visit cultural landmarks like the Stortinget and the National Theatre, and experience the lively atmosphere day and night. | **GPS Coordinates:** 59.91322528026106, 10.741290054547374

The Oslo Fjord is a picturesque inlet in southeastern Norway that spans approximately 120 kilometers from the _small village of Bonn_ to the _bustling city of Oslo_. Carved by glaciers during the last ice age, it features a stunning landscape with lush forests, charming towns, and colorful cabins. The fjord is divided into the inner and outer sections - **_The inner Oslo_** Fjord is characterized by its urban surroundings, hosting the city of Oslo, with cultural and historical landmarks. In contrast, **_the outer Oslo_** Fjord features more pristine and remote landscapes, showcasing natural beauty and diverse ecosystems. With over 400 islands, each holding unique historical significance, the fjord is a hub for outdoor activities like swimming, kayaking, and boating in the summer, while winter brings ice skating and fjordside saunas.

The best way to explore the Oslofjords depends on your preferences and desired experience! Here are some options to consider:

1. Fjord Cruises: Choose from 2-hour to full-day fjord cruises featuring traditional sailing ships, electric boats, or cruises with seafood buffets.

Inner fjord tours showcase charming islands and towns, while outer fjord excursions offer dramatic cliffs and open sea views.

2. Island Hopping: Explore islands like Hovedøya with Viking history, Gressholmen's former fortress, or Bleikøya with beaches and hiking trails using public ferries or private water taxis.

3. Kayaking: Get close to the water by renting kayaks or joining guided tours, suitable for both beginners and experienced kayakers. Paddle around islands, discover hidden coves, and spot marine life.

4. Hiking and Cycling: Hike scenic trails on Bygdøy peninsula or Langøyene island, or bike through forests and coastal areas with breathtaking views. Combine these activities with shore picnics for an outdoor adventure.

5. Sauna Boat Tours: Embrace Nordic tradition on a sauna boat tour, enjoying fjord scenery while warming up in a cozy sauna and taking a refreshing dip in the cool water.

6. Fishing Trips: Join fishing tours catering to all skill levels, providing equipment and guidance. Experience the tranquility of open water and the thrill of a successful catch.

FJORD CRUISING WITH BATSERVICE SIGHTSEEING

The most recommended experience is an Oslo Fjord cruise, offered year-round with various operators such as *RIB Oslo* and *Norway Yacht Charter*. **Båtservice Sightseeing** (*https://nyc.no/boatservice-sightseeing*, **GPS Coordinates:** 59.91095360018847, 10.73164451534262), affiliated with Norway Yacht Charter, stands out as a cost-effective choice with diverse tour options, including themed cruises. The evening boat tour with a three-hour sail and all-you-can-eat shrimp buffet is highly recommended. Båtservice Sightseeing provides standard tours year-round, with varying daily departures. Winter cruises are limited to weekends. The cost starts at 439 kroner (about $42.67) per person, with a 15% discount for Oslo Pass holders. Departures are mostly from the pier near **_Oslo City Hall_**.

3. AKERSHUS FORTRESS

Akershus Fortress stands as a historical monument in Oslo, Norway, constructed in 1299 and serving diverse roles over the centuries, from a medieval castle to a royal residence and military stronghold. Today, this site is a favored destination for tourists, offering not only captivating views of the city but also housing museums, cultural events, and serene green spaces.

GPS Coordinates: 59.907725838939946, 10.73707336803989 | **Time to Spend:** 2 hours to Half Day | **Operating Hours:** 6:00 AM to 9:00 PM | **Admission:** Free | Fees apply for museums and guided tours.

Reasons to Explore it: Engage with the well-preserved medieval castle ruins, providing an immersive experience into the city's rich history. | Visit the Norwegian Armed Forces Museum and the Resistance Museum to delve into Norway's past. Attend concerts or exhibitions hosted within the fortress grounds. | Take in the sweeping panoramas of Oslo and the Oslo Fjord from the fortress's ramparts. | Unwind in the lush Akershus Castle Park, a verdant haven ideal for picnics and leisurely strolls.

How to get there: The fortress is easily accessible on foot, by tram, or bus from Oslo city center, with a short walk from the National Theater and Aker Brygge.

What to do there: Tour the medieval chambers, ascend the Akershus Tower, and visit the Royal Mausoleum. | Delve into Norway's military and resistance history at the dedicated museums. | Enjoy concerts, theatrical performances, or open-air movie screenings in the fortress courtyard. | Discover hidden corners, capture photos from scenic viewpoints, and relax in the park. | Indulge in lunch or dinner with breathtaking fjord panoramas at restaurants situated within the fortress.

TIPS

Free Tours: Join summer tours to uncover the fortress's history.

Concert Vibes: Experience vibrant summer concerts at Akershus.

Picnic Paradise: Enjoy a leisurely lunch in Akershus Park with a picnic basket. | *Hidden Charm:* Discover the medieval beauty of Akershus Castle Chapel, featuring exquisite stained glass windows.s

4. THE ROYAL PALACE (DET KONGELIGE SLOTT)

King Carl Johan conceived a majestic residence befitting his reign, and construction commenced in 1825. Finalized in 1849, the Palace has borne witness to numerous generations of monarchs, hosting grand state occasions and quiet family moments alike. Today, it stands as the official residence of the present King and Queen, with the Crown Prince residing at Skaugum in

Asker.

Location: Slottsplassen 1, 0010 Oslo, Norway | **_Operating Hours:_** Open to visitors during the summer | **_Ticket Prices:_** Adults: 175, Seniors/students: 145, Wheelchair (all ages): 125, Children (6–18): 125, Children 0–5: free, Closed groups of up to 40 persons: NOK 5500 | _Combination tickets for the Royal Palace and Queen Sonja Art Stable:_ Adults: 265, Seniors/students: 215, Children: 165, The prices include a ticket fee of NOK 25 | **_Official Website:_** _https://www.kongehuset.no/seksjon_ | _https://www.royalcourt.no_ | **GPS Coordinates:** 59.917483782013555, 10.72741981534262 | **Time to Spend:** 1 to 2 Hours

THINGS TO DO AND SEE

Witness the Changing of the Guard: Daily at 1:30 PM (May to September), observe the vibrant and precisely choreographed ceremony as the Royal Guards switch duties—an essential Oslo experience!

Explore the Palace Park: Wander through the lush gardens, crafted in an English landscape style, featuring serene ponds, concealed sculptures, and breathtaking panoramic views of the city and fjord. | **_Admire the architecture:_** Take in the imposing facade, adorned with intricate stuccowork and sculptures. Notice the lions guarding the main entrance and the Royal Balcony, where the King and Queen make appearances on special | **_Peek into the State Apartments (through guided tours):_** Enter the opulent realm of Norwegian royalty during the summer months. Marvel at the extravagantly decorated halls, chandeliers, and priceless artworks. | **_Attend a Royal Event:_** If fortunate enough to visit during a special occasion, witness the splendor and pageantry of a Royal Wedding, Baptism, or State Visit. Check the Royal Court website for upcoming events.

TIPS

Book guided tour tickets online: Skip the lines and secure your spot by pre-booking, especially during peak seasons. | **_Pack a picnic:_** Set up a blanket in the Palace Park and relish a delightful lunch surrounded by greenery and stunning views. | **_Wear comfortable shoes:_** The Palace grounds are extensive, so be prepared for some walking to explore all the hidden gems. | **_Visit during the Christmas season:_** Experience the Palace illuminated in festive splendor, with a magnificent Christmas tree adorning the main entrance. | *Learn some Norwegian phrases:* A few basic greetings and "takk" (thank you) will go a long way in showing respect and endearing yourself to the locals.

5. THE NORWEGIAN OPERA & BALLET

In 1957, the vision of having a dedicated opera and ballet venue in Norway took root. Following years of meticulous planning and construction, the impressive architectural gem situated in Bjørvika harbor was revealed to the public in 2008. Its slanted, white granite exterior, reminiscent of glaciers meeting the sea, has since become an iconic symbol of Oslo.

Address: Kirsten Flagstads Plass 1, 0150 Oslo, Norway | *Architecture firm:* Snøhetta | *Capacity:* 1,400 | *Opened:* 12 April 2008 | *Operating Hours:* Monday - Friday: 10:00 AM - 8:00 PM, Saturday - 11:00 am to 6:00pm | Sunday: 12:00 PM - 6:00 PM | *Admission:* A general admission ticket for a guided tour of Oslo Opera House costs 130 NOK (or around $11.80 USD), with discounts available for seniors and under 30s. Refer to the website for the latest pricing details: *https://www.operaen.no/en/booking/booking-information* | *Official Website:* https://www.operaen.no/en | *GPS Coordinates:* 59.908077442127784, 10.752680630685244 | **Time to Spend:** 2 Hours to Half a day

THINGS TO DO AND SEE

Immerse Yourself In The Enchantment Of Opera And Ballet: Witness the skill of the Norwegian National Opera and Ballet on stage, presenting a repertoire that spans timeless classics to contemporary productions for an unforgettable experience. | *Explore The Architectural Marvel:* Take a guided tour or wander independently through the awe-inspiring spaces of the Opera House. Admire the grand foyers, the horseshoe-shaped auditorium, and the breathtaking views from the rooftop. | *Ascend The "Opera Mountain":* Hike or take the scenic elevator to the apex of the sloping roof, a popular spot for enjoying the city's beauty and the fresh air. | *Have A Picnic In The Opera Park:* Bring a blanket and some snacks, and relax on the lush green lawns surrounding the Opera House. It's an ideal spot for leisure and people-watching. | *Dine With A View:* Indulge in a delectable meal at one of the Opera House's restaurants, offering stunning vistas of the Oslo fjord and the city skyline.

TIP

Book Early: Secure your seats in advance for popular performances that sell out quickly. | **_Dress Smart:_** Opt for smart casual attire for evening performances, although no strict dress code applies. | **_Fjord Combo:_** Enhance your visit by combining it with a fjord cruise departing from the Opera House. | **_Free Performances:_** Check the website for occasional free outdoor events on Opera Plaza. | **_Learn Norwegian:_** Familiarize yourself with basic phrases to connect with locals.

- Bonus Tip: Attend "Opera on the Beach" in summer for a magical experience —an open-sky opera with the Oslo fjord as your backdrop!

6. VIGELAND PARK

Gustav Vigeland dedicated over 40 years of his life, starting in 1907, to the creation of Vigeland Park. His aim was to establish a space that mirrored the entire spectrum of human experience, spanning from carefree childhood to the inevitable twilight of our days. The outcome is a captivating voyage through life's stages, immortalized in stone and bronze.

Location: Frognerparken, Nobels gate 32, 0268 Oslo, Norway | **_Operating Hours:_** Accessible 24/7, all year round. While the park itself is free to enter, specific attractions within the park may have distinct opening hours and fees. | **_Admission:_** Free access to the park and most sculptures. The Vigeland Museum (situated within the park) charges an entrance fee of NOK 80 for adults, NOK 40 for students and seniors, and free entry for children under 6. | **_Official Website:_** _https://vigeland.museum.no/en/vigelandpark_ | **GPS Coordinates:** 59.92744834461648, 10.700993746027862 | **Time to Spend:** 1 to 2 Hours

WHY VIGELAND PARK IS WORTH VISITING

The Monolith: Climb the 17-meter monolith, a towering granite spiral representing the circle of life and the continuous ascent towards spiritual enlightenment. | **_The Wheel of Life:_** Observe the poignant cycle of birth, death, and rebirth portrayed in the intricate bronze ring, serving as a stark reminder of life's impermanence. | **_The Angry Boy:_** Experience the intense emotion radiating from this iconic statue, symbolizing childhood frustration and the universal struggle against limitations. | **_The Children's Playground:_** Unleash your inner child amidst the playful bronze sculptures of children engaged in various states of amusement and mischief. | **The Bridge:** Leisurely stroll along the 100-meter bridge adorned with 58 sculptures, each showcasing a unique facet of human interaction and emotion. | **Hidden Gems:** Keep a lookout for concealed treasures like the bronze frogs nestled among the foliage, adding a touch of whimsical delight to your exploration.

TIPS

Time Your Visit: Opt for early mornings or late evenings to avoid crowds and bask in the enchanting light on the sculptures. | *Picnic Paradise:* Enjoy a leisurely lunch on the lush lawns surrounded by art and nature. | *Guided Insights:* Deepen your understanding with guided tours, available in various languages. | *Hands-On Experience:* Respectfully touch the sculptures; Vigeland intended them to be experienced up close. | *Embrace Surprises:* Explore hidden corners for unexpected charms beyond the well-trodden paths.

7. THE IBSEN MUSEUM

The Ibsen Museum in Oslo, Norway, housed in Henrik Ibsen's final residence, offers a captivating journey through the literary giant's life and works. Founded in 1900 and restored in 2006, the museum showcases exhibits like "Henrik Ibsen - Contrary to All Expectations," providing insights into his impact on Norwegian literature. Explore Ibsen's meticulously preserved apartment, personal library, and letters. The museum hosts lively events, fostering a vibrant community and ensuring Ibsen's legacy inspires audiences worldwide, making it a must-visit for literature enthusiasts and culture seekers alike. | *WHY IT IS WORTH VISITING:* The museum provides an intimate experience, allowing visitors to explore his meticulously preserved apartment, personal library, and letters. The exhibits offer insights into Ibsen's life, thoughts, and creative process, making it a captivating destination for literature enthusiasts. The museum's lively events and commitment to fostering a community of learners ensure that Ibsen's legacy continues to inspire and challenge audiences worldwide. | *WEBSITE:* *https:// ibsenmt.no/en*

8. THE VIKING SHIP MUSEUM (VIKINGSKIPSHUSET)

Established in 1926, the Viking Ship Museum embarked on a groundbreaking mission to preserve and showcase extraordinary vessels, standing today as a tribute to Viking craftsmanship and the enduring allure of these seafaring warriors.

Location: Huk Aveny 35, 0287 Oslo, Norway | *Operating Hours:* Regrettably, the Viking Ship Museum is presently closed for extensive renovations until late 2026/early 2027. While the ships are temporarily inaccessible, you can still explore Viking Age exhibitions at the Historical Museum in central Oslo. You can Stay updated on the reopening and future exhibitions through the Vikingtidsmuseet website: *https://www.vikingtidsmuseet.no/ english* | *Admission Prices:* Admission prices for the Viking Ship Museum will be disclosed upon its reopening. Check the museum's website closer to the opening date for updated information. | *Entrance to the Historical Museum's Viking Age exhibitions* is presently NOK 110 for adults, NOK 70 for students/seniors, and free for children under 16. | *Official Website: https:// www.vikingtidsmuseet.no/english* | GPS Coordinates: 59.90540746175145, 10.6844075 | | **Time to Spend:** 1 to 2 Hours

<u>WHAT TO DO AND SEE (WHEN THE MUSEUM REOPENS)</u>

Marvel at the Magnificent Ships: Encounter the Oseberg ship, Tune ship, and Gokstad ship—each a testament to Viking ingenuity and craftsmanship. Learn about their history, construction techniques, and the captivating lives they led on the high seas. | *Explore the Burial Treasures:* Immerse yourself in the realm of Viking rituals and beliefs through a rich collection of grave goods found alongside the ships. From weapons and tools to jewelry and textiles, these artifacts provide insight into the daily lives and cultural practices of these ancient warriors. | *Discover the Viking Age:* Delve beyond the ships and explore the broader Viking world. Gain knowledge about their trading networks, navigation skills, and mythology through interactive exhibits, multimedia presentations, and informative displays. | *Witness the Craftsmanship:* Visit the museum's workshops, where skilled artisans demonstrate traditional Viking crafts such as shipbuilding and wood carving. You might even have the opportunity to try your hand at some Viking-inspired activities! | *Enjoy the Views:* Take a break from your Viking adventures and appreciate the beautiful surroundings. Situated on the

Bygdøy peninsula, the museum offers stunning views of the Oslo fjord and surrounding islands.

TIPS

Plan Your Visit: Check the website for updated opening hours, ticket prices, and events closer to the museum's reopening. | ***Explore Bygdøy's Attractions:*** The Viking Ship Museum is just one of many on the peninsula. Visit the Norwegian Maritime Museum, Kon-Tiki Museum, or Fram Museum for a full day of maritime adventures. | ***Pack a Picnic:*** Enjoy the beautiful setting with a picnic on the museum grounds. Benches and grassy areas offer a relaxing atmosphere. |

MUSEUMS

Established in 1936, the Fram Museum pays homage to the adventurous spirit of Norwegian polar explorers. At its core lies the "Fram," an iconic polar exploration vessel that braved three arduous expeditions, including Nansen's epic drift across the Arctic Ocean and Amundsen's triumphant race to the South Pole. Stepping onto the meticulously preserved Fram is akin to a journey back in time, with the echoes of pioneering voyages lingering in the creaking timbers.

Location: Bygdøynesveien 37, 0288 Oslo, Norway | **Operating Hours:** Daily: 10:00 AM - 5:00 PM (May - September) | Tuesday - Sunday: 10:00 AM - 4:00 PM (October - April) | Closed Mondays (except public holidays) | **Admission Prices:** Adults: NOK 140 (approximately USD 15) | Children (6-15 years): NOK 70 (approximately USD 7) | Families: NOK 325 (approximately USD 35) | Free entry with Oslo Pass | **Official Website:** https://frammuseum.no | **GPS Coordinates:** 59.903542676866, 10.699707539203889 | | **Time to Spend:** 2 Hours to Half a day.

THINGS TO SEE & DO

Explore the "Fram": Climb aboard the renowned ship and venture into its cramped cabins, galley, and engine room. Envision the icy winds on the deck, the constant hull creaking, and the crew's unwavering determination. | **Polar Adventure Exhibitions:** Immerse yourself in gripping tales of Norwegian polar exploration through interactive exhibits, captivating artifacts, and multimedia presentations. Discover the scientific breakthroughs, technological innovations, and human determination that conquered the frozen expanses. | **Meet the Arctic Animals:** Encounter stuffed polar bears, walruses, seals, and penguins, gaining insights into their adaptations to the harsh polar environment. | **Temporary Exhibitions:** The museum regularly hosts intriguing temporary exhibitions exploring various facets of polar exploration, history, and science. Check their website for current offerings.

Combine Your Visit: Take advantage of combo tickets to explore other museums on the Bygdøy peninsula, including the Viking Ship Museum, the Kon-Tiki Museum, and the Norwegian Maritime Museum.

2. HOLMENKOLLEN SKI MUSEUM AND TOWER

Holmenkollen's history dates back to the 12th century, transforming into a hub for winter sports in the 19th century. The Ski Museum, founded in 1923, stands as the world's oldest institution dedicated to this thrilling discipline. Its displays span centuries of skiing evolution, showcasing the progression from rudimentary wooden planks to state-of-the-art Olympic equipment. The tower, constructed in 1892, has witnessed numerous ski jumps, evolving into a cherished symbol of Oslo.

Location: Holmenkollbakken 40, 0380 Oslo, Norway | ***Operating Hours:*** Museum: Tuesday-Sunday 10:00 AM - 4:00 PM (closed Mondays) | Tower: Daily 10:00 AM - 8:00 PM (weather permitting) | ***Admission Prices:*** *Museum & Tower Combo:* NOK 180 (Adults), NOK 100 (Children 6-15 years) | Museum only: NOK 120 (Adults), NOK 60 (Children 6-15 years) | Tower only: NOK 120 (Adults), NOK 60 (Children 6-15 years) | ***Official Website:*** *https://www.skiforeningen.no/en/holmenkollen* | ***GPS Coordinates:*** 59.96432614936464, 10.667072296880256 | | **Time to Spend:** 1 to 2 Hours

THINGS TO SEE & DO

Museum: Take a chronological journey through Norwegian skiing history. View historical skis, attire, and artifacts, gaining insights into the cultural significance of the sport. Interactive exhibits and multimedia presentations bring the past to life. | ***Tower:*** Ride the elevator to the observation deck, where panoramic views of Oslo and the surrounding fjords await. Envision the jumps of Olympic champions from this spot and feel the exhilaration of the leap. | ***Ski Simulator:*** Test your virtual skiing skills on the Holmenkollen Simulator, experiencing the thrill of descent without the icy chill. Challenge your friends and determine who reigns supreme on the slopes! | ***Souvenir***

Shop: Grab a unique memento from your Holmenkollen adventure at the on-site shop. Discover traditional Norwegian crafts, sports apparel, and keepsakes that capture the essence of Oslo. | **Cafe:** Recharge at the cozy cafe after your explorations, enjoying panoramic views and delectable refreshments. Indulge in a warm waffle with jam, a classic Norwegian treat, or sip on hot chocolate for a truly hygge experience.

TIPS

Combine Your Visit with Holmenkollen Park: Explore the expansive park surrounding the museum and tower, featuring hiking trails, cross-country skiing tracks, and breathtaking natural beauty.

Check the Event Calendar: Holmenkollen frequently hosts sporting events and cultural gatherings. Plan your visit around exciting competitions or festive celebrations. | **Purchase a Combo Ticket:** Save money and enjoy both the museum and tower with a combined ticket. | **Consider Public Transportation:** Easily reach Holmenkollen by metro (Holmenkollen station) or bus (lines 30 and 33). Skip the car and enjoy the scenic ride up the hill.

3. THE MUNCH MUSEUM

The reimagined Munch Museum, unveiled in 2021, serves as a testament to the profound impact of the artist's legacy. In 1944, Edvard Munch entrusted his extensive collection, comprising over 28,000 works, to Oslo. Although the original museum, established in 1963, fulfilled its purpose, there was a longing for a space that truly reflected the magnitude of Munch's influence. The result is a stunning architectural marvel along the Oslo waterfront—a 13-floor structure pulsating with artistic energy.

Location: Edvard Munchs plass 1, 0194 Oslo, Norway. | **Opening Hours:** Sun-Tue: 10:00 AM - 6:00 PM | Wed-Sat: 10:00 AM - 9:00 PM

Prices: Adults: NOK 250 (approximately $25 USD) | Students/Seniors: NOK 180 (around $18 USD) | Children under 18: Free | **Website:** https://www.munchmuseet.no/en | **GPS Coordinates:** 59.90672485433143, 10.75574711534262 | **Time to Spend:**

WHAT TO SEE & DO

Scream, Scream, Scream: Yes, "The Scream" is here—not just one, but four versions! Witness the iconic angst firsthand and feel the reverberations of existential tremors. | ***Beyond the Screams:*** Munch's brilliance extends beyond one masterpiece. Explore the museum's 13 floors, each teeming with paintings, prints, photographs, and even Munch's personal artifacts. Immerse yourself in melancholic landscapes, confront the raw vulnerability of his portraits, and let the vibrant colors dance before your eyes. | ***Than Munch:*** The museum isn't just a repository for the master's works. Temporary exhibitions featuring contemporary artists in dialogue with Munch offer a fresh perspective, fostering conversations across generations and artistic movements.

TIPS

Audio Guides: Enhance your experience with insightful audio guides, available in multiple languages. Let Munch's own words and the curators' interpretations provide a deeper understanding of his art. | ***Restaurant and Cafe:*** Recharge after your emotional journey at the museum's in-house restaurant or cafe. Indulge in delicious Norwegian cuisine with breathtaking fjord views—an ideal way to decompress and reflect on the artistic depths you've explored. | ***Book in Advance:*** Tickets can sell out, particularly during peak seasons. Secure your spot online to avoid disappointment and ensure a seamless entry into Munch's world. | ***Embrace the Stroll:*** The Munch Museum is a brief walk from the Oslo Opera House and Aker Brygge waterfront. Lace up your walking shoes and enjoy a scenic stroll, immersing yourself in the city's vibrant atmosphere.

4. NATURAL HISTORY MUSEUM

Step back into the year 1814, the genesis of the museum, originally known as the University Botanical Garden. Evolving over two centuries, it has transformed into a splendid complex showcasing captivating exhibits on zoology, geology, and climate change. Presently, it proudly holds the title of Norway's largest natural history collection, featuring over 6 million objects narrating tales of our planet's diverse history.

Location: Sars' gate 1, 0562 Oslo, Norway. | *Operating Hours:* Tuesday - Sunday: 10:00 AM - 5:00 PM | Closed on Mondays | *Admission Prices:* Adults: NOK 160 (approximately $16) | Children (aged 6-17): NOK 80 (approximately $8) | Free admission for children under 6 years old | Family ticket   2+4= NOK 420 (approximately $42) | *Website:* https://www.nhm.uio.no/english | *GPS Coordinates:* 59.920271708730446, 10.771007454547894 | | **Time to Spend:** 1 to 2 Hours

THINGS TO SEE AND DO

Dinosaur Adventure: Journey back to the era of giants, encountering a colossal T-Rex skeleton, fossilized footprints, and insights into these prehistoric behemoths. | *Dioramas Come Alive:* Immerse yourself in stunning recreations of Norway's landscapes, showcasing taxidermied animals in their natural habitats, from icy tundra to lush rainforests. | *Minerals that Sparkle:* Marvel at the dazzling world of minerals, featuring glittering crystals, colorful gemstones, and meteorites, unveiling Earth's hidden treasures. | *A Tropical Paradise:* Escape the Nordic chill in the vibrant Botanical Garden, home to exotic plants from around the world, housed in greenhouses filled with life, from delicate orchids to towering cacti. | *Climate Change Challenge:* Engage with interactive exhibits shedding light on the urgent issue of climate change, exploring its impact on our planet and discovering ways to protect it for future generations.

TIPS

Free Family Sundays: Every Sunday, families with children under 16 enjoy free admission, offering a budget-friendly and enriching experience. | *Guided Tours:* Enhance your visit with guided tours, available in English and Norwegian, providing deeper insights into exhibits and the museum's history. | *Pack a Picnic:* Enjoy a leisurely lunch break in the peaceful Botanical Garden, remembering to dispose of waste responsibly. | *Combine and Conquer:* Conveniently located near other attractions like the Munch Museum and Vigeland Park, plan your day to explore multiple cultural gems in one go. | *Embrace the Outdoors:* After your museum adventure, take a stroll through the charming Grünerløkka district, known for its trendy cafes, independent shops, and vibrant street art.

5. NORWEGIAN MUSEUM OF CULTURAL HISTORY

Established in 1894, the museum originated as a modest collection of rural artifacts. Over time, it evolved into an expansive complex featuring more than 150 relocated buildings from various regions of Norway. Each structure narrates tales of everyday life, ranging from fishermen's cottages to grand manor houses, providing a captivating glimpse into the nation's rich heritage.

Location: Museumsveien 10, Bygdøy, 0287 Oslo, Norway | *Accessibility:* Take picturesque ferry ride across the Oslofjord, followed by a brief stroll through lush parklands. | *Opening Hours And Fees:* Hours and operation and admission fees varies according to season of the year, chech *https:// norskfolkemuseum.no/en/hours-fees-directions* for full details of operating hours and admission fee. | *Website: https://norskfolkemuseum.no/en* | **GPS Coordinates:** 59.91178399371873, 10.686875262282538 | | **Time to Spend:** 2 Hours to Half a day

<u>THINGS TO SEE AND DO</u>

Open-Air Enchantment: Explore a living history book with over 150 relocated buildings representing various regions and eras. Visit a bustling 19th-century market square, step into a traditional Sami turf hut, or marvel at the intricate carvings of a majestic stave church. | *Costumes that Captivate:* Immerse yourself in a kaleidoscope of colors and textures at the costume and textile exhibition. Admire intricately embroidered folk costumes, elegant ball gowns, and practical workwear, each piece telling stories of celebrations, everyday life, and cultural identity.

Viking Splendor: Experience the world of legendary seafarers at the Viking Ship Hall. Admire the well-preserved Oseberg Ship with intricate carvings and a fascinating burial chamber. Learn about Viking voyages, myths, and daily lives. | *Modern Moments:* The museum extends beyond the past, showcasing contemporary Norwegian culture through engaging temporary exhibitions. Explore themes like sustainable living, urban development, and artistic expression, gaining a deeper understanding of modern Norway. | *Family Fun:* Let young explorers unleash their imaginations at interactive workshops and play areas. Dress up in traditional costumes, build miniature houses, or enjoy captivating storytelling sessions. Family Sundays offer free admission and special activities for all ages.

TIPS

Combine and Conquer: Explore the Bygdøy peninsula's cultural gems, including the Viking Ship Museum, the Kon-Tiki Museum, or the Fram Museum for a comprehensive historical experience. | ***Pack a Picnic:*** Enjoy a leisurely lunch amidst the serene beauty of the museum grounds. Find a cozy spot near the open-air buildings or in the Botanical Garden for an al fresco experience. | ***Embrace the Audio Guide:*** Enhance your visit with the informative audio guide, available in several languages, providing insights into exhibits, buildings, and the museum's history. | ***Free Days:*** Take advantage of free admission on the second Tuesday of every month for a budget-friendly exploration. | ***Seasonal Charm:*** Witness the museum grounds transform throughout the year, from blooming flowers in spring to vibrant open-air demonstrations in summer, warm hues of autumn, and a magical snowy backdrop in winter.

6. THE KON-TIKI MUSEUM (KON-TIKI MUSEET)

In 1947, the intrepid Norwegian adventurer Thor Heyerdahl embarked on an apparently insurmountable journey aboard the Kon-Tiki, a modest raft crafted from balsa wood using ancient techniques. His ambitious mission was to traverse the vast Pacific Ocean, demonstrating the feasibility of cultural exchange between Polynesia and South America. Heyerdahl's audacious undertaking captivated the global imagination, leading to the establishment of the Kon-Tiki Museum in 1949. The museum serves as the home for the iconic raft and the narrative of his extraordinary adventure.

Location: Bygdøynesveien 36, 0286 Oslo, Norway | ***Accessibility:*** Take a scenic ferry voyage across the Oslofjord, followed by a brief stroll through lush parklands, guiding you to the Kon-Tiki Museum's entrance. | ***Opening Hours:*** Monday - Sunday: 10:00 AM - 5:00 PM
Admission Prices: Adults: 140, Children (ages 6–17): 50, Families (2+5): 300, Groups (min. 10): 100, Seniors: 100, Students: 50 (all prices in NOK) | ***Website:*** *https://kon-tiki.no* | ***GPS Coordinates:*** 59.90386258193901, 10.698109346027865 | | **Time to Spend:** 1 to 2 Hours

THINGS TO SEE AND DO

Face-to-Face with Kon-Tiki: The main attraction is the original Kon-Tiki raft. Marvel at this humble vessel that successfully navigated the formidable Pacific, appreciating its ingenious construction and imagining the challenges and triumphs of Heyerdahl's crew. | *Beyond the Raft:* The museum offers more than just the Kon-Tiki. Explore captivating exhibits featuring Heyerdahl's other daring expeditions, including Ra, the papyrus reed boat that crossed the Atlantic, and Tigris, a Mesopotamian reed boat that sailed the Arabian Sea. | *Dive into Archaeology:* Put on your metaphorical Indiana Jones hat and delve into exhibits detailing Heyerdahl's archaeological discoveries. Learn about his expeditions to Easter Island, the Galapagos Islands, and Peru, where he unearthed ancient secrets and challenged established archaeological theories. | *More Than Just Artifacts:* The Kon-Tiki Museum goes beyond showcasing the past, aiming to inspire the future. Interactive exhibits explore themes of sustainability, cultural exchange, and environmental awareness, encouraging visitors to connect Heyerdahl's adventures to contemporary issues. | F*amily Fun:* Allow young explorers to embark on their own adventures with engaging activities and workshops. Build miniature rafts, solve puzzles inspired by Heyerdahl's journeys, and listen to captivating storytelling sessions that breathe life into history.

TIPS

Explore Bygdøy's cultural hub: Kon-Tiki Museum, Viking Ship Museum, Norwegian Maritime Museum, and Fram Museum offer a comprehensive historical adventure. | *Opt for the insightful audio guide*, available in multiple languages, enhancing your visit with commentary on exhibits, Heyerdahl's journeys, and the museum's history. | *Create a picnic paradise:* Pack a delightful lunch and enjoy it amid the serene beauty of the museum grounds. Find a cozy spot by the water or under the trees for an al fresco experience. | *Free Days:* Explore the museum on a budget with free admission every second Tuesday of the month. | *Channel Your Inner Explorer*: Snap numerous Instagram-worthy photos at the museum, posing with the Kon-Tiki and capturing the scenic beauty of Bygdøy.

7. THE NATIONAL MUSEUM (NASJONALMUSEET)

Established in 1830 as a humble assortment of paintings, the National Museum has evolved into a cultural powerhouse, featuring two distinguished structures: a grand 19th-century palace exhibiting classical art and a modern, well-lit building housing contemporary treasures. Each venue exudes its unique charm, inviting exploration into the progression of Norwegian artistry.

Locations: Brynjulf Bulls plass 3, 0250 Oslo, Norway | *Opening Hours:* Sunday, thursday, friday and saturday: 10am–17pm, Monday: Closed, Tuesday and wednesday: 10am–8pm | *Admission Prices:* *Adult:* NOK 200, *Under 25 years of age:* NOK 120, *Student under 30 years of age:* NOK 120, *Children and youth (0–17):* NOK 0, *Companion:* NOK 0 | *Website:* *https://www.nasjonalmuseet.no/en* | *GPS Coordinates:* 59.91203311451723, 10.729418861370483 | | **Time to Spend:** 1 to 2 Hours

THINGS TO SEE AND DO

Embrace the Masters: Encounter iconic works by Edvard Munch, the renowned artist behind "The Scream," and appreciate the captivating landscapes of J.C. Dahl. Immerse yourself in the golden age of Norwegian painting, where vibrant colors and dramatic scenes narrate the stories of the nation's soul. | *Dive into Design:* Unravel the intricate tapestries of Norwegian craftsmanship, from intricately carved furniture to breathtaking silverwork. Witness the evolution of design trends and the enduring connection between everyday objects and artistic expression. | *Contemporary Encounters:* Enter the sleek, light-filled space of the new building and engage with thought-provoking contemporary art installations, multimedia presentations, and interactive exhibits that blur the lines between observer and participant. | *A Global Tapestry:* Explore the influence of international artistic movements beyond Norway's borders. From ancient Egyptian artifacts to Renaissance paintings, the museum weaves a narrative of cultural exchange and the shared language of human creativity. | *Family Fun:* Catering not only to adults, the National Museum offers interactive games, hands-on workshops, and storytelling sessions designed to spark children's imaginations and foster a lifelong love for art.

TIPS

Free Days: Utilize the opportunity for free admission on the second Tuesday of every month to explore the museum on a budget. | *Embrace the Audio Guide:* Enhance your visit with the informative audio guide, available in multiple languages, providing insightful commentary on exhibits, artists, and the museum's history.

Pack a Picnic: Enjoy a leisurely lunch amidst the serene beauty of the National Museum's gardens. Find a cozy spot in the sunshine or under the shade of trees for a delightful al fresco experience. | *Seasonality and Special Events:* Keep an eye on the museum's website for information on seasonal exhibitions, concerts, and family events throughout the year, offering fresh perspectives and unique experiences for every visit.

8. THE NATIONAL GALLERY (NASJONALGALLERIET)

Established in 1836, the National Gallery embarked on a mission to amass and exhibit artistic excellence. Originally situated within the Royal Palace, it relocated to its grand edifice in 1882, subsequently becoming a renowned landmark for both its artistry and architectural significance. Today, while integrated into the larger National Museum of Art, Architecture, and Design, it maintains its distinct identity as a sanctuary for fine art.

Location: Brynjulf Bulls plass 3, 0250 Oslo, Norway | *Operating Hours:* Sunday, thursday, friday and saturday: 10AM–5PM, Monday: Closed, Tuesday and wednesday   10–8PM Special opening hours for specific exhibitions; refer to the website for details. | *Admission Prices:* Adult: NOK 200, Under 25 years of age: NOK 120, Student under 30 years of age: NOK 120, Children and youth (0–17): NOK 0, Companion: NOK 0 | *Official Website:* https:// www.nasjonalmuseet.no/en/visit/locations/the-national-museum | **GPS Coordinates:** 59.911968570332164, 10.729075538629514 | **Time to Spend:** 1 to 2 Hours

WHAT TO DO AND SEE

Encounter Nordic Masters: Immerse yourself in the masterpieces of Norway's artistic luminaries, including Edvard Munch's iconic "The Scream," Hans Dahl's captivating landscapes, and Christian Krohg's poignant social commentary. | *Explore International Gems:* Traverse time and continents through masterworks by Rembrandt, Monet, Cézanne, Goya, and numerous others. The collection spans centuries and movements, fostering a truly global artistic dialogue.

Uncover Hidden Treasures: Move beyond the prominent names and uncover the lesser-known works that carry their own narratives. Each room holds surprises, with each brushstroke offering a potential avenue for personal connection. | **_Join a Guided Tour:_** Deepen your understanding of the art with a guided tour, available in English and various other languages. Learn about the artists, techniques, and historical context, enriching your overall experience. | **_Relax and Reflect:_** Take a respite in the enchanting Sculpture Garden, surrounded by tranquil greenery and contemporary art installations. It provides an ideal setting to contemplate what you've encountered and let your own creativity flourish.

TIPS

Book Tickets Online: Skip the queues and secure your tickets in advance, especially during peak seasons. | **_Combine Your Visit with Other National Museum Locations:_** Oslo's cultural panorama extends beyond the National Gallery. Explore the Architecture and Design Museum and the Munch Museum for a comprehensive artistic adventure. | **_Free Thursdays:_** Take advantage of free admission on Thursdays after 6:00 PM to partake in the vibrant Thursday Night program, featuring talks, music, and special events. | **_Pack a Picnic:_** Enjoy a leisurely lunch before or after your visit in the picturesque Sculpture Garden. | **_Leave Your Bags at the Cloakroom:_** Facilitate your exploration of the galleries by depositing your bulky belongings at the cloakroom for a small fee.

9. ASTRUP FEARNLEY MUSEET

Astrup Fearnley Museet is a modern art museum situated in a striking building designed by Renzo Piano on Tjuvholmen island. It offers breathtaking fjord views and features a dynamic collection of contemporary art.

Address: Tjuvholmen 2, 0277 Oslo, Norway | **_GPS Coordinates:_** 59.907335489105655, 10.721510784657378 | **_Website:_** _https:// www.afmuseet.no/en_

WHY YOU SHOULD VISIT

Contemporary Art Hub: Explore an eclectic collection of international contemporary art, including works by Jeff Koons, Cindy Sherman, and emerging artists. | *Architectural Masterpiece:* The museum's glass and steel structure seamlessly integrates with the fjord setting, creating a luminous and inspiring space. | *Rotating Exhibitions:* Engage with new voices and artistic trends through a continuous series of temporary exhibitions challenging and provoking thought. | *Waterfront Location:* Enjoy stunning fjord views from the museum's rooftop terrace, providing an ideal setting for contemplation after exploring the art.

10. THE NOBEL PEACE CENTER (NOBELS FREDSSENTER)

Borne out of the vision of Nobel Peace Prize laureate Ragnar Frisch, the Center commenced its operations in 2005. Its primary objective is to amplify the voices of laureates, foster peace education, and empower individuals to serve as catalysts for positive change.

Location: Brynjulf Bulls plass 1, 0250 Oslo, Norway | *Founded:* 2005 | *Architect:* David Adjaye | *Operating Hours:* Tuesday through Sunday between 11 a.m. and 5 p.m. From May 1 to Aug. 31, the property also opens its doors on Mondays. | *Admission Prices:* Adults: NOK 160, Students/ Seniors: NOK 100, Children under 18: Free, Free admission on Fridays after 4:00 PM | *Official Website:* https://www.nobelpeacecenter.org/en | *Coordinates:* 59.912027984521785, 10.7305412 | | **Time to Spend:** 1 to 2 Hours

WHAT TO DO AND SEE

Meet the Laureates: Immerse yourself in the narratives of peacemakers through interactive exhibits, multimedia presentations, and personal artifacts. From the resolute activism of Malala Yousafzai to the environmental commitment of Wangari Maathai, each laureate's journey sparks hope and potential. | *Confront Global Challenges:* Explore urgent issues such as climate change, conflict resolution, and human rights through engaging displays and activities. The Center encourages critical thinking, fostering open discussions and challenging visitors to be part of the solution. | *Climb the "Nobel Mountain":* Ascend the roof via a hike or the scenic elevator, experiencing a captivating space for reflection and enjoying panoramic views of Oslo's harbor and cityscape. Envision holding the world's weight with the iconic City Hall at your feet, akin to what laureates do on Nobel Prize Day.

| *Join a Guided Tour:* Delve deeper into the Center's exhibits and mission with a guided tour, offered in English and various other languages. Learn about the Peace Prize's history, the selection process, and the ongoing work of the laureates. | *Participate in Events:* Attend a documentary screening, join a lecture by a renowned peace activist, or participate in a workshop on peacebuilding and conflict resolution. The Center hosts a vibrant array of events, providing opportunities to connect with like-minded individuals and amplify one's voice for peace.

TIPS

Book Tickets Online: Skip the queues and secure your spot by booking tickets in advance, especially during peak seasons. | *Combine Your Visit with Other Oslo Attractions:* The Center is conveniently located within walking distance of the Akershus Fortress and the City Hall, making it an ideal stop during your exploration of Oslo. | *Free Fridays:* Take advantage of complimentary admission on Fridays after 4:00 PM to engage in the lively Friday Night program featuring talks, music, and special events. | *Grab a Coffee and Reflect:* Enjoy a cup of coffee or a light lunch in the Center's cafe, offering views of the harbor and the bustling city. It's the perfect spot to digest newfound insights and plan your next peacemaking action. | *Support the Cause:* Consider making a donation to the Center's initiatives, contributing to the amplification of peacemakers' voices globally. Every contribution, regardless of size, makes a meaningful impact.

11. NORWEGIAN MUSEUM OF SCIENCE AND TECHNOLOGY

Fondly called "Teknisk Museum." With over 25 permanent exhibits showcasing transportation history, medical advancements, oil and gas, music machines, and more, the museum is a captivating experience for all ages. | You can Engage in hands-on exploration at the Oslo Science Centre, where experiments with electricity, light, sound, bridge-building, robot racing, and cosmic exploration await in an interactive haven. | You can Witness the world's oldest steam roller, a historic 1878 machine symbolizing ingenuity. The museum hosts diverse temporary exhibitions on scientific and technological themes. | For a family-friendly outing, the museum provides interactive exhibits, play areas, and a café.

Address: Kjelsåsveien 143, 0491 Oslo, Norway. | *Recommended visit duration:* 2-3 hours. | *Operating hours:* Tue, Wed, Fri: 9am - 4pm | Thu: 9am - 7pm | Sat-Sun: 10am - 5pm | Closed Mondays | *Admission fees:* Adults: NOK 190 (approx. $20) | Children (6-17 years): NOK 125 (approx. $13 | Free with Oslo Pass | *Website:* https://www.tekniskmuseum.no | GPS Coordinates: 59.9667477767344, 10.782369572717514

PARKS

A distinct part of Frogner Park, Vigeland Park merits separate recognition for its unique artistic significance, hosting Gustav Vigeland's monumental sculpture collection depicting the human lifecycle.

Location: Kirkeveien 50, 0272 Oslo, Norway | **GPS Coordinates:** 59.9305° N, 10.7312° E | **Website:**

WHY VIGELAND PARK IS WORTH VISITING

Artistic Masterpiece: Immerse yourself in Vigeland's emotive sculptures exploring themes of love, family, and existential struggles. The iconic Monolith, a 17-meter granite pillar, is a poignant highlight. | **Unique Architectural Elements:** Beyond sculptures, the park features captivating architectural elements like the bronze entrance gate and the Monolitten Bridge, offering panoramic views. | **Historical Significance:** As the world's largest single-artist sculpture collection, Vigeland Park provides insight into Gustav Vigeland's creative genius and profound impact on Norwegian art.

2. FROGNER PARK (FROGNERPARKEN)

Frogner Park stands as the largest central park in Oslo, featuring a charming combination of peaceful green expanses, lively flowerbeds, and an intriguing open-air sculpture museum.

Location: Kirkeveien 50, 0272 Oslo, Norway | **GPS Coordinates:** 59.9305° N, 10.7312° E | **Website:**

WHY FROGNER PARK IS WORTH VISITING

Vigeland Sculpture Park: Housed within Frogner Park, the renowned Vigeland Sculpture Park exhibits over 200 sculptures by Gustav | **Serene Atmosphere:** Whether for a leisurely picnic, a refreshing jog in lush green surroundings, or contemplative moments amid sculptures, Frogner Park provides a tranquil escape from the city's hustle. | **Diverse Activities:** Catering to various interests, the park offers opportunities for sunbathing, picnicking, playing Frisbee, and enjoying open-air concerts.

3. EKEBERGPARKEN

Situated atop Ekeberg Hill, this sculpture park offers stunning city views and an eclectic array of modern and contemporary artworks.

Location: Kongsveien 59, 0191 Oslo, Norway | *GPS Coordinates:* 59.9082° N, 10.7745° E | *Website:*

WHY EKEBERGPARKEN IS WORTH VISIT

Modern Art Haven: Encounter thought-provoking sculptures by international artists like Louise Bourgeois, Damien Hirst, and Tony Cragg, seamlessly blending art with nature. | *Panoramic Vistas:* Revel in breathtaking views of Oslo's skyline and the Oslofjord from various points within the park. | *Tranquil Escape:* While not as expansive as Frogner Park, Ekebergparken offers an intimate and secluded setting, ideal for a peaceful stroll amidst art and nature.

4. ST. HANSHAUGEN PARK (ST. HANSHAUGEN)

A traditional urban park renowned for its picturesque views, romantic landscapes, and historical allure.

Location: Knud Knudsens plass 5, 0442 Oslo, Norway | *GPS Coordinates:* 59.9458° N, 10.7508° E | *Website:* https://www.visitoslo.com/en/product/?TLp=15920)

WHY ST. HANSHAUGEN IS WORTH VISITING

Panoramic views of Oslo can be savored from the hilltop Festplassen. | *A romantic ambiance* is created by winding paths, charming bridges, and a serene duck pond. | *Boasting a rich history* dating back to the 1850s, the park features delightful historical elements such as the Tårnhuset tower. | *It serves as a popular venue* for outdoor concerts and events, particularly during the summer months.

5. BIRKELUNDEN PARK

A dynamic and vibrant park celebrated for its sense of community, diverse recreational activities, and artistic atmosphere.

Location: Birkelunden 4, 0354 Oslo, Norway | *GPS Coordinates:* 59.9190° N, 10.7706° E | *Website:* *https://www.fleamarketinsiders.com/oslo-flea-market-birkelunden-marked-grunerlokka*

WHY BIRKELUNDEN PARK IS WORTH VISITING
A lively environment featuring a playground, basketball court, and skateboard park. | *A hub for artists and musicians*, contributing to a vibrant creative atmosphere. | *Hosts open-air cinema and flea markets*, adding excitement during the summer months. | *Home to charming cafes and restaurants*, providing a perfect setting for a leisurely coffee break.

6. BOTANICAL GARDEN (BOTANISK HAGE)
An idyllic haven for plant enthusiasts, showcasing diverse flora from around the globe and emphasizing environmental awareness.

Location: Sars' gate 1, 0562 Oslo, Norway | *GPS Coordinates:* 59.9391° N, 10.7540° E | *Website:* *https://www.nhm.uio.no*

WHY BOTANISK HAGE IS WORTH VISITING
Houses over 7,000 plant species from various regions and climates, including a Japanese garden and tropical greenhouses. | *Stunning flower displays* throughout the year, particularly during the vibrant spring and summer seasons. | *Educational exhibits and guided tours* offer insights into plant diversity and conservation. | *A tranquil oasis within the city*, providing an ideal space for a peaceful stroll or a relaxing picnic.

7. TØYEN PARK (TØYENPARKEN)
A vast expanse of grassy hills adorned with large trees, Tøyen Park is a favored destination for recreation, festivals, and birdwatching.

Location: Tøyengata 2A, 0185 Oslo, Norway | *GPS Coordinates:* 59.9205° N, 10.7553° E | *Website:*

WHY TOYEN PARK IS WORTH VISITING
Scenic views complemented by the Øyafestivalen music festival. | The Tøyenbadet swimming complex, featuring both indoor and outdoor pools,

enhances the park's appeal.

8. SOFIENBERG PARK (SOFIENBERGPARKEN)

Sofienberg Park is a lush green space featuring ponds, sculptures, a rose garden, playground, and historical significance.

Location: Hammersborggata 2, 0179 Oslo, Norway | *GPS Coordinates:* 59.9329° N, 10.7410° E | *Website:* https://www.oslo.kommune.no/natur-kultur-og-fritid/tur-og-friluftsliv/parker-og-friomrader/sofienbergparken

WHY SOFIENBERG PARK IS WORTH VISITING
Scenic beauty combined with historical monuments. A popular spot for picnics and relaxation.

9. AKERSHUS FORTRESS AND CASTLE PARK (AKERSHUS FESTNING)

A medieval fortress with a rich historical legacy, Akershus Fortress offers museums, panoramic views, and hosts public events.

Location: Akershusstranda 50, 0150 Oslo, Norway | *GPS Coordinates:* 59.9472° N, 10.7308° E | *Website:* https://forsvaret.no/om-forsvaret/tjenestesteder/oslo)

WHY AKERSHUS FORTRES & CASTLE PARK IS WORTH VISITING
Historical significance intertwined with museums. | Breathtaking city and fjord views, along with engaging public events.

10. BYGDØY ROYAL MANOR PARK (BYGDØY KONGSGÅRD)

Surrounding a royal estate, Bygdøy Royal Manor Park offers picturesque landscapes, beaches, historical buildings, museums, and various recreational activities.

Location: Bygdøyveien 81, 0290 Oslo, Norway | *GPS Coordinates:* 59.9228° N, 10.6803° E | *Website:* https://www.kongsgardpark.no

WHY BOTANISK HAGE IS WORTH VISITING
Rich royal history complemented by beaches and historical buildings. |

Museums, hiking trails, and diverse recreational activities enhance the park's allure.

11. PALACE PARK

A charming public park surrounding the Royal Palace of Oslo, offering majestic trees, manicured lawns, and tranquil ponds.
Address: Akersgata 50, 0017 Oslo, Norway | GPS Coordinates: 59.9105° N, 10.7369° E | Website: https://www.tripadvisor.com/Attraction_Review-g190479-d5549686-Reviews-The_Palace_Park-Oslo_Eastern_Norway.html

WHY THE PALACE PARK IS WORTH VISITING
Near the Royal Palace, experience a serene park setting with glimpses of royal architecture. | ***Immerse yourself in history*** dating back to the 1840s, offering a haven for both royalty and the public. | ***Enjoy natural beauty*** with well-maintained grounds, mature trees, reflecting ponds, and picturesque landscapes, taking a break from city bustle. | ***Explore Queen's Park***, an enclosed section featuring a Rococo garden dating back to 1751. | ***Discover hidden gems*** like sculptures by Norwegian artists and commemorative monuments. The park is easily accessible by foot, bike, or public transportation from central Oslo.

12. TJUVHOLMEN SCULPTURE PARK

An open-air art space on the former island of Tjuvholmen, showcasing contemporary sculptures amidst a dynamic harbor setting.

Address: Tjuvholmen allé 46, 0279 Oslo, Norway | ***GPS Coordinates:*** 59.9089° N, 10.7737° E | ***Website:*** *https://www.nasjonalmuseet.no*

WHY TJUVHOLMEN SCULPTURE PARK IS WORTH VISITING
Immerse in a unique art experience with a dynamic collection of contemporary sculptures by international and Norwegian artists. | ***Enjoy the vibrant harborside atmosphere***, offering scenic views of boats and the Oslo skyline. | ***Explore freely with no admission fees***, making it family-friendly with interactive sculptures and open spaces for children. | ***Easily accessible*** by ferry, bus, or bike from central Oslo. | ***Enhance your art immersion*** by combining your visit with exploring the nearby Astrup Fearnley Museum of Modern Art.

13. STUDENTERLUNDEN

Studenterlunden is a delightful and historically significant park offering a refreshing green haven amidst the urban bustle near Karl Johans gate. Popular among students from the nearby University of Oslo, it holds a legacy dating back over 150 years.

Location: Karl Johans gate 47, 0113 Oslo, Norway | *GPS Coordinates:* 59.9105° N, 10.7383° E | *Website:*

WHY STUDENTERLUDEN IS WORTH VISITING
Historic Hub: With over a century of significance, the park played a role in Norway's 19th-century quest for independence. | *Scenic Oasis:* Adorned with mature trees, flowerbeds, and a charming fountain, the park offers a peaceful escape. | *Cultural Gem:* Home to the National Theatre of Norway, the park hosts open-air performances and events, especially in the summer. | *Central Convenience:* Located in Oslo's heart, easily reachable by foot, bike, or public transport, making it an ideal city exploration stop. | *Relaxation Haven:* Whether for picnics, reading under a tree, or people-watching, Studenterlunden provides a laid-back atmosphere to unwind.:

14. KAMPEN PARK

Kampen Park, situated in the trendy Kampen neighborhood of Oslo, is a vibrant and compact park boasting stunning city views, a charming rose garden, and a lively atmosphere.

Location: Bøgata 28, 0368 Oslo, Norway | *GPS Coordinates:* 59.9299° N, 10.7691° E | Website:

WHY KAMPEN PARK IS WORTH VISITING
Hilltop Views: The park offers stunning panoramas of Oslo's skyline, fjord, and neighboring areas. | *Enchanting Rose Garden:* A delightful spot with fragrant blooms, especially captivating in the summer. | *Vibrant Gathering Hub:* Locals flock to the park for sunbathing, frisbee, picnics, and lively outdoor activities. | *Family-Friendly Features:* The park includes a playground for kids and a skatepark for teenagers. | *Hipster Haven:* Situated in Kampen,

a trendy neighborhood known for colorful houses, independent shops, and stylish cafes, enhancing the overall charm.

NEIGHBORHOODS

Oslo, the captivating capital of Norway, extends beyond its famed Viking ships and fjords. Its vitality emanates from a tapestry of diverse neighborhoods, each pulsating with its unique character and allure. Join us on a curated journey through five distinctive corners of Oslo, where hidden gems and local flavors await to enhance your exploration.

1. GRÜNERLØKKA

Once a working-class enclave, this district has transformed into a trendy haven for hipsters, artists, and students. Immerse yourself in vintage boutiques, street art, and eclectic cafes such as Tim Wendelboe, a coffee haven celebrated by coffee aficionados.

Hidden Jewel: Blå, an iconic music venue nestled in an old tram depot, hosts intimate performances from emerging artists. | *Local Delicacies*: Dive into *Mathallen*, a lively food hall bursting with global flavors, or grab a falafel roll from *Falafel Kingen*, a Grünerløkka institution.

2. AKER BRYGGE

Once an industrial harbor, Aker Brygge has evolved into a chic playground for luxury yachts, designer shops, and waterfront dining.

Must-Visit: The Astrup Fearnley Museum of Modern Art houses a collection of contemporary masterpieces, while Akershus Fortress provides captivating fjord views and a journey through medieval history. | *Local Tastes:* Indulge in fresh seafood at *Fiskeriet*, or savor gourmet tapas at *Barceloneta.*

3. FROGNER

Frogner is full of Upscale streets adorned with grand villas that lead to the iconic *Vigeland Park*, a vast sculpture garden showcasing Gustav Vigeland's expressive bronze figures.

Cultural Highlights: Frogner House features contemporary art, while the Nobel Peace Center delves into peacebuilding initiatives.

Fine Dining: Treat yourself to a Michelin-starred experience at Maaemo, or relish an elegant brunch at Frogner Kro.

4. GAMLE OSLO

Gamle Oslo is Oslo's historic core, where cobbled streets wind past the 12th-century *Oslo Cathedral* and the delightful *Medieval Park*.

Historical Exploration: Visit the Viking Ship Museum for a glimpse into the city's maritime history or Akershus Castle for royal intrigue.

Local Flavors: Recharge with a pastry at the renowned Ostehuset Galleri, or enjoy fish and chips with a twist at Fiskeriet.

5. HANSHAUGEN PARK

Escape the urban hustle in this lush retreat offering panoramic vistas and scenic trails. Pack a picnic and bask in the sun alongside locals.

Hidden Marvel: St Hanshaugen Memorial Grove, situated atop the hill, pays homage to World War II heroes through a poignant sculpture. | **Refreshment Choices**: Grab a coffee at Kaffebrenneriet or savor homemade ice cream at Isoteket Hanshaugen.

6. MAJORSTUEN

Majorstuen emanates a refined atmosphere, boasting grand villas, upscale boutiques, and trendy cafes. Yet, beneath the chic exterior lies a bohemian spirit, with vintage treasures like *Fretex (clothing)* and *The Thief (books)* nestled amidst designer stores.

Highlights: Explore Frognerparken, a sprawling oasis adorned with sculptures, and traverse Bogstadveien, Oslo's premier shopping avenue. | **Hidden Gem:** Discover **Tilt**, a retro arcade bar where you can sip cocktails and embrace your inner gamer.

7. BYGDØY

Bygdøy peninsula unfolds as an open-air museum where Viking sagas intertwine with lush parklands. Immerse yourself in the Viking Ship Museum, showcasing majestic vessels from the 9th century, or delve into maritime history at the Norwegian Maritime Museum.

Highlights: Must-visit sites include *The Viking Ship Museum* and the *Fram Museum*, which exhibits polar exploration vessels. | **Hidden Gem:** Find serenity at *Hakkejernbakken*, a secluded beach offering breathtaking fjord views and an escape from the city bustle.

8. GRØNLAND

Grønland vibrates with multicultural energy, where Pakistani spices blend with Turkish coffee aromas, and vibrant sari shops line lively streets. This district is a haven for budget-conscious travelers and culinary enthusiasts seeking exotic flavors.

Highlights: Explore _Olaf Ryes Plass market_, a lively bazaar teeming with fresh produce and international delicacies, and marvel at the _Islamic Cultural Centre's_ stunning architecture. | **Hidden Gem:** Indulge in the city's best Turkish kebabs at _Dønner Kebab House_, a no-frills eatery.

9. KVADRATUREN

Kvadraturen, Oslo's historic core, weaves a tapestry of cobbled streets and grand squares. The Royal Palace, Parliament building, and Oslo Cathedral stand as guardians of the city's past, while contemporary art galleries and trendy cafes infuse a modern touch.

Highlights: Visit Akershus Fortress, a medieval castle offering panoramic city views, and stroll Karl Johans gate, Oslo's bustling main street. | **Hidden Gem:** Experience the charm of _Ellingtons konditori_, a bakery serving traditional Norwegian pastries since 1855.

10. TJUVHOLMEN

Once a notorious prison island, Tjuvholmen has evolved into an enclave of contemporary art and innovative architecture. Renowned museums like Astrup Fearnley Museet and the Munch Museum grace the sleek waterside apartments and Michelin-starred restaurants.

Highlights: Explore Astrup Fearnley Museet, showcasing modern and contemporary art, and stay at the design masterpiece Thief Hotel with breathtaking harbor views. | **Hidden Gem:** Uncover season-changing popup cafes and galleries, offering a glimpse into Oslo's vibrant art scene.

11. CITY CENTER

Oslo's vibrant core pulsates with historical richness, cultural allure, and contemporary delights. Uncover the 17th-century _Akershus Castle_, meander through the splendid _Royal Palace Gardens_, or catch a show at the iconic _Oslo_

Opera House.

Hidden Treasure: Explore *Bogstadveien*, Oslo's foremost shopping street, and venture into *Kunstnernes Hus*, a discreet gem presenting contemporary art exhibitions. | ***Local Culinary Delights:*** Indulge in a treat from the renowned *Strømstangen Bakery* or relish Norwegian specialties like *brunost (brown cheese)* and *fiskekaker (fish cakes)* at the lively *Mathallen food hall*.

12. STREET ART AT INGENS GATE

Immerse yourself in Oslo's vibrant street art scene. Ingens gate, a cobblestone alley near Akerselva River, transforms into an open-air gallery with ever-evolving murals and installations.

Hidden Jewel: Follow the *Frognerelva Sculpture Promenade*, a scenic riverside path adorned with quirky and thought-provoking sculptures. ***Local Flavor:*** Grab a coffee and a cinnamon bun at the cozy *Kaffebrenneriet* or indulge in a delectable vegan burger at Bunuel Oslo.

13. TØYEN

This diverse neighborhood hums with a blend of students, locals, and immigrants. Explore the vibrant Tøyen Park, visit the Islamic Cultural Center, or peruse the eclectic shops on Åsengata.

Hidden Gem: Immerse yourself in Turkish culture at Hamam Oslo, a traditional Turkish bathhouse offering steamy relaxation and massages. | ***Global Cuisine:*** Savor authentic Vietnamese delights at Pho Bo or embark on a culinary journey at Maaemo, a Michelin-starred restaurant pushing the boundaries of Nordic gastronomy.

14. VULKAN NEIGHBORHOOD

This former shipyard has morphed into a trendy hotspot with a cool, industrial atmosphere. Discover contemporary art galleries, independent boutiques, and lively nightlife venues.

Hidden Gem: Attend a concert or performance at Vulkan Arena, a live music venue housed in a converted grain silo. | ***Local Pleasures:*** Enjoy craft beers and street food at Mathallen Vulkan or sip cocktails with fjord views at Kampen Bistro.

15. BJØRVIKA

Oslo's latest district is a dynamic blend of modern skyscrapers, green expanses, and waterfront promenades. Experience the iconic Oslo Opera House, explore the Astrup Fearnley Museum of Modern Art, or unwind on the lush rooftop park of MUNCH.

Hidden Jewel: Rent a kayak and paddle around the harbor for a unique perspective of the city skyline. | *Harborside Delights:* Savor fresh seafood at Fiskeriet or indulge in upscale dining with panoramic views at Eataly Oslo. Hidden Oasis: Discover serenity in the concealed haven of St. Hanshaugen Memorial Grove, dedicated to honoring heroes of World War II with poignant sculptures.

Local Pleasures: Indulge in a Michelin-starred dining experience at Maaemo, or relish an elegant brunch at Frogner Kro.

SOME FAST FACTS ABOUT OSLO NEIGHBORHOODS

Elegant Boulevard: Bygdøy Allé in Frogner is renowned for its tree-lined charm, upscale architecture, high-end shops & restaurants.

Family-Friendly Enclaves: Majorstuen, Frogner, and Nordre Aker are popular for families, offering peace, quality schools, and proximity to parks and amenities.

Prestigious, Yet Pricey: Frogner stands out as Oslo's most expensive neighborhood, boasting upscale residences, proximity to parks, embassies, and high-end amenities.

Affordability in Grønland: Grønland is Oslo's more affordable choice, providing a multicultural vibe, diverse dining, and reasonably priced housing compared to upscale areas.

Medieval Charm: Gamlebyen (Old Town) is Oslo's oldest neighborhood, dating back to medieval times. Explore historical buildings, cobblestone streets, and remnants of medieval fortifications.

Hipster Haven in Grünerløkka: Grünerløkka is Oslo's hipster hub, featuring trendy cafes, bars, vintage shops, and art galleries. Embrace a vibrant atmosphere and diverse cultural events in this creative community.

WALKING OSLO

Length of Walk: 4 km

Important places covered in this walk are: (1) The Palace Park (2) The Royal Palace (3) Oslo City Hall - (4) Akershus Fortress (5) Vippa Oslo (6) SALT (7) The Norwegian National Opera & Ballet (8) Operastranda in Bjørvika (9) MUNCH (10) Nimbu (11) Koie Ramen Munch (12) Talormade Oslobukta (13) [Vin] Bjørvika

Commence your walk in the serene Royal Palace Park, where you can leisurely traverse beautiful greenery, explore the Ingrid Alexandra Sculpture Park, and marvel at the majestic Royal Palace itself. If you arrive at 13:30, you might even witness the changing of the guards ceremony in front of the palace. | ***Head towards the waterfront***, guided by the unmistakable Oslo City Hall with its two distinctive red brick towers, offering both a landmark and a worthwhile visit. Inside and outside the building, you'll find impressive artwork and commissions by renowned artists, including Edvard Munch. | ***Continue to Akershus Fortress overlooking the fjord***, a historic site present for nearly 700 years. Proceed to Vippa, a spacious food hall offering a diverse range of global cuisines. | ***Follow the waterfront to SALT***, a venue combining art, music, and saunas to create a delightful space for leisure and entertainment. Enjoy a concert or relax in the sauna. | ***The iconic Oslo Opera House***, with its marble structure seemingly floating in shallow water, stands out prominently on the waterfront. The rooftop is a popular spot for relaxation. | ***Explore the fjord swimming spots near the Opera***, including the recently opened beach, Operastranda, favored by locals for cooling down on warm summer days. | ***Visit MUNCH***, a new waterfront museum dedicated to Edvard Munch's art. Alongside stunning artwork, discover cafes, restaurants, and engaging cultural events. | ***Conclude your waterfront exploration at one of the numerous bay-side restaurants***. Consider trying modern spicy Indian cuisine at *Nimbu* (59.90634836512157, 10.760326796875432), relishing ramen delights at *Koie Ramen Munch* (59.90678301636227, 10.755998424444435), or savoring exquisite doughnuts at Talormade

Oslobukta (59.906697932002885, 10.75751504743351). | [Vin] Bjørvika (59.90671, 10.75575) is a wine bar where you can choose from an extensive selection of wines with the assistance of knowledgeable staff members.

2. EXPLORE GRÜNERLØKKA LIKE A LOCAL

Length of Walk: 3-4 km
Important places covered in this walk are: (1.) Botanical Garden - (2.) Grünerløkka Brygghus - (3.) Velouria Vintage (4.) Haralds Vaffel - (5.) Frøken Dianas Salonger - (6.) Mathallen Food Hall (7.) Ingensteds (8.) Blå - (9.) SYNG

Commence your journey with a leisurely walk through the Botanical Garden (Botanisk hage), surrounded by magnificent trees and beautiful blooms. Take a break at the charming café nestled in the heart of the garden for a cup of coffee and a delectable pastry. | *Transition to the vibrant Grünerløkka neighborhood* for a mix of shopping, tasty snacks, and delightful drinks. *Dive into Liebling*, an independent café that not only serves excellent coffee but also provides a cozy setting for playing board games. As you venture further into Grünerløkka, explore the Grünerløkka Brygghus microbrewery, boasting an impressive array of beers. Grünerløkka is a paradise for enthusiasts of vintage attire and unique niche stores! | *Discover your next fashion statement* at *Velouria Vintage* or Frøken Diana's Salonger, and don't miss the captivating handmade pottery and jewelry at BRUDD. If you find yourself in need of an energy boost during your shopping spree, indulge in the delectable waffles at Harald's Vaffel, a true Oslo favorite. | *Cross the Akerselva river and head towards Vulkan*, where the *Mathallen food hall* awaits with a plethora of dining options. | *Continue your journey to Ingensteds and Blå*, neighboring venues along the riverbank known for hosting various concerts and events, including a *Sunday flea market*. | *Conclude your evening* on a high note at SYNG, a lively karaoke bar!

3. ART AND CULTURE WALK

Length: 6 km
Important places covered in this walk are: (1) Astrup Fearnley Museet - (2) Fineart Oslo - (3) The Queen Sonja Art Stable - (4) Kunstnernes Hus - (5) House of Literature (Litteraturhuset) - (6) Lofthus Samvirkelag Kunstnernes Hus -

(7) Gallery Albin Upp - (8) The Vigeland Museum - (9) Vigeland Sculpture Park - (10) Anne på landet – (12) Frognerparken

Initiate your journey at the _Astrup Fearnley Museum_, situated along the waterfront, where you can immerse yourself in outstanding contemporary art and marvel at the striking architecture crafted by the renowned architect Renzo Piano. | Just a brief stroll away, **discover Fineart Oslo**, the largest art gallery in Norway. | **Proceed to the Royal Palace Park**, where The Queen Sonja Art Stables, once the Palace's stables, now host rotating exhibitions from the Royal Art Collection. | **On the opposite side of the Royal Palace Park** lies _Kunstnernes Hus_, an artist-operated museum showcasing Norwegian and international contemporary art. If you're feeling peckish, indulge in delectable pizza at _Lofthus Samvirkelag_ within the gallery or opt for a literary-inspired meal at the House of Literature. | Following this, **take a leisurely stroll through the serene Briskeby neighborhood** behind the Royal Palace and venture to _Galleri Albin Upp_, housed in a 19th-century farmhouse. Enjoy a meal or drink at the gallery's café. | **Meander through broad, tree-lined avenues** past vibrant apartment buildings until you reach the _Vigeland Museum_, offering insights into the works of Norway's renowned artist, Gustav Vigeland. Cross the road to enter the _Vigeland Sculpture Park_, a must-see destination in Oslo. Don't miss the iconic Sinnataggen (Angry Boy) statue, located in the middle of the park. | **For a century-old building experience**, visit _Anne på Landet_, a charming café perfect for coffee and snacks. | **To conclude your art-filled journey**, head towards the city centre and reach the _Majorstuen metro station_.

4. FJORDSIDE FOODIE & OPERA WALK

Length: 4 Kilometers
Important places covered in this walk are: (1) The Tiger (2) Deichman Bjørvika / Oslo Public Library, Main Branch (3) The Norwegian National Opera & Ballet (4) Operastranda in Bjørvika (5) Åretak - Viking Rowboat Rental (6) Sørenga (7) Mirabel (8) IKI: Sørenga Social Club (9) Bun's Burger Bar

Commence your journey at the renowned Tiger statue located at Jernbanetorget, right in front of Oslo Central Station. Proceed towards the remarkable Deichman Bjørvika public library, a newly constructed architectural marvel. | **_Continue your exploration_** to the Oslo Opera House by the fjord, where you can take a stroll on its distinctive roof. | **_En route to Sørenga, discover Oslo's latest beach_**, _Operastranda_, and a popular hangout spot known as _Sukkerbiten_. Here, you can relish food, savor a beer, partake in events, or indulge in a sauna session with Oslo Fjord Sauna. For an authentic Viking experience, consider renting a _færing_, a traditional Norwegian rowboat, to explore the Oslo fjord. | **_Cross the walkway to enter the revitalized neighborhood of Sørenga_**, celebrated for its popularity as a sunbathing and swimming destination in the fjord. Treat yourself to a delightful lunch at various restaurants in the area. _Mirabel_ offers Mediterranean-inspired cuisine, _Sørenga Social Club_ boasts excellent seasonal and locally sourced ingredients, and don't miss the delectable dim sum at _Hakkaiza_ or the gourmet burgers at _Bun's Burger Bar._

HIKING OSLO

Oslo seamlessly integrates with nature, with a significant portion of the city comprising protected forests, hills, and lakes. Convenient public transport links connect the city to a variety of hiking trails, catering to all skill levels just beyond the urban center. Even within the bustling city, one can swiftly transition to a peaceful forest environment, surrounded by the sounds of birds. Whether you're on a brief visit or an extended stay in Oslo, embarking on a hike is easily accessible. The hiking options range from easy to challenging, ensuring there's a suitable trail for everyone. Remarkably, you could explore the forest for three consecutive weeks without retracing your steps. Below I highlight some of the top hiking trails in and around Oslo:

1. SOGNSVANN LAKE

Sognsvann Lake provides a haven for recreation, offering ideal locations for picnics, swimming, fishing, and leisurely walks. To combine history and hiking, take metro line 5 to Sognsvann. Upon arrival, explore the gravel trail encircling the lake, a preferred choice for picnickers and swimmers. Opt for a slightly more challenging route, suitable for beginners, by following the 5km (3mi) trail that winds into the forest, unveiling the peaceful Nedre Blanksjø lake hidden among the trees. This undiscovered gem signifies the geographical center of Oslo municipality, providing an ideal escape from the city's hustle and bustle. For those reluctant to leave the serenity behind, follow the trail from Sognsvann to ascend to the summit of Vettakollen mountain. The panoramic view from the summit is genuinely awe-inspiring, showcasing extensive areas of Oslo, the Oslo fjord, its coastline, and numerous small islands.

2. NORDMARKA FOREST

Nature enthusiasts will find bliss in Nordmarka Forest, where a variety of wildlife, including foxes, beavers, moose, deer, eagles, and hares, may be observed during hikes. To reach this natural haven, take a 30-minute metro ride from downtown Oslo to Frognerseteren and then follow the blue trails (as the red trails are reserved for skiing in winter). The approximately 14km (8.7mi) trail leading to Sørkedalen requires around six hours, allowing for a leisurely lunch break in one of the charming café cabins along the route. While the walk is quite extensive, it is not strenuous. The terrain is mainly flat through the forest, without steep inclines. Afterwards, you can conveniently take the bus back to the metro and return to the city center.

3. FROGNERSETERN

This 5km (3mi) trek is an excellent walk for beginners, catering to individuals of all skill levels and offering breathtaking vistas of Oslo. Board the Frognerseteren metro line to Lillevann, where you'll be treated to scenic views of rural Oslo before descending to the renowned *Frognersetern Restaurant*. Established in 1891, this venue provides an ideal setting to savor traditional Norwegian dishes (don't miss the meatballs and sour cream porridge) while enjoying a panoramic view of the city below. Following the meal, continue along a segment of the 50km (31mi) trail that passes by Midtstubakken, Holmenkollen Chapel, and a toboggan run dating back to the first Luge World Championship in 1955. According to Einar, "The highlight of this hiking journey undoubtedly lies in the majestic Holmenkollen ski jump, one of the most renowned sports arenas globally."

4. KROKSKOGEN

"If you're up for a real challenge, this is the trail to tackle," advises Einar. "It's genuinely thrilling, presenting some challenging sections, but the beauty is exceptional. It's advisable to join a tour group if possible, given that it's approximately a 45-minute drive from Oslo." The 25km (15.5mi) hike commences at the stunning Mørkgonga nature reserve, where a narrow gorge was carved millions of years ago. The journey then leads through the Krokskogen forests, passing by Lake Nibbitjern and ascending the steep Gyrihaugen mountain. Einar notes, "The view from the summit, overlooking the fjords and mountains, is truly magnificent. If completed in a day, the hike takes about eight hours, including transportation by bus. Therefore, it's essential to bring provisions like food and water and wear hiking shoes capable of withstanding wet conditions."

5. KOLSÅSTOPPEN

For an intermediate-level hike spanning approximately 8km (5mi), venture to Kolsåstoppen, a popular wooded mountain located roughly 12km (7.5mi) from Oslo's city center. Utilize the 150 bus from Oslo to Stein Gård, and proceed towards the entrance of the Stein Gård farm to access the beginning of the hike. This trek, lasting around two hours, meanders through a captivating forest and alongside a small lake, providing an opportunity for a refreshing swim in warm weather. However, it's advisable to apply ample mosquito repellent. According to Einar, "During this hike, you'll ascend two peaks and enjoy a panoramic view of Oslo, Bærum, and the Oslo Fjord."

6. ØSTMARKA FOREST

Encompassing an extensive 256 square kilometers (100 sq mi) in the eastern part of Oslo, Østmarka Forest features an intricate network of hiking trails that meander past vast lakes and through majestic pine groves. To commence your exploration, take metro line 3 (Mortensrud) to Ulsrud station. From there, follow the 8km (5mi) trail heading southward to Mariholtet Sportsstue, a café nestled deep within the forest, providing an ideal setting for a quick hot chocolate break. Along your journey, contemplate taking a invigorating swim in one of the lakes, ascend rocky ridges for sweeping views of the forest, or simply relax on one of the secluded lake beaches. Opt to either loop back or extend your adventure further to uncover additional treasures within the forest, including the charming Nøklevann Lake.

7. MELLOMKOLLEN

Referred to as Oslo's equivalent to the Alps, Mellomkollen mountain offers an excellent day trip for intermediate hikers seeking a break from the city center. The trail spans approximately 12km (7.5mi) and requires three to four hours to traverse, guiding hikers past the glistening Øyungen Lake and through the scenic Nordmarka Forest before culminating in a climb up the mountain. Upon reaching the plateau, cross the marsh to enjoy uninterrupted views over Oslo. To reach Mellomkollen from the city, take the 54 bus (Kjelsås) to Godals vei, then transfer to the 51 bus (Maridalen) and travel to the final stop, Skar. Note that return buses depart from Skar only once an hour, so it's essential to be aware of the schedule to avoid a lengthy wait after completing your hike.

8. VETTAKOLLEN

Rising above Sognsvann lake, Vettakollen promises panoramic vistas and a sense of accomplishment. The moderately challenging 4km trail ascends from the lake, meandering through dense forest before emerging onto the open mountainside. At the summit, a breathtaking 360-degree panorama unfolds, showcasing Oslo, the Oslofjord, and a tapestry of islands. For an added challenge, continue to the neighboring peak of Korketrekanten, known for its rugged rock formations and stunning views.

9. GREFSENKOLLEN

This 5km loop trail is ideal for nature enthusiasts seeking a leisurely escape. Take the T-bane (metro) to Storo and follow the forested path uphill. Breathe in the fresh air as you traverse the scenic trails, passing vibrant wildflowers and quaint cabins. As you reach the summit, be rewarded with panoramic views of Oslo and the surrounding valleys. Enjoy a picnic on the grassy slopes or grab a bite at the Grefsenkollen Restaurant, where traditional Norwegian fare awaits.

10. KING'S VIEW

Steeped in history, this 8km trail offers a glimpse into Oslo's royal past. Start at Frognerseteren station and follow the gravel path used by King Haakon VII during his daily walks. The trail winds through lush forests and charming meadows, eventually reaching the aptly named King's View. This scenic viewpoint, favored by the king for its sweeping vistas of the city and the Oslofjord, provides a perfect spot for a photo break or a contemplative moment.

11. MØRKGONGA

Calling all adventure seekers! This 25km trek through the Mørkgonga nature reserve is a true test of stamina and will. Embark on this challenging journey from the Lillomarka station, venturing into the wild and ancient forests. Navigate narrow gorges carved by glaciers millions of years ago, scale the steep Gyrihaugen mountain, and be awestruck by the fjord and mountain panoramas from the summit. Remember, this hike is best tackled with proper gear, provisions, and possibly a tour group for safety and guidance.

TOURS

1. *Taste of Oslo Walking Tour*: Discover Oslo's lively neighborhoods on this walking tour, pausing at local hotspots to savor traditional Norwegian cuisine and snacks. Immerse yourself in the city's culture and history while indulging in delicious food—a perfect experience for food enthusiasts seeking a deep dive into the local scene. This tour starts from $135 USD per adult and can be booked on viator here: *https://bit.ly/48VbtYH*

2. *Guided Oslo Fjord Cruise by Silent Electric Catamaran:* Embrace the serenity of a Norwegian fjord as you embark on a peaceful cruise along the Oslo Fjord during your visit to Oslo. Drift along the tranquil and profound waters, observing the wildlife and picturesque natural surroundings on both fjord banks, including the sighting of islands. This tour is perfect for nature enthusiasts and those fascinated by the beauty of Norwegian fjords. It holds particular appeal for children and caters to all age groups. Immerse yourself entirely in the experience, with expansive floor-length panoramic windows aboard, ensuring unobstructed views of the fjord throughout the journey. Whether you prefer the cozy interior or the refreshing outside deck, the cruise offers a fully immersive experience for everyone. This tour starts from $59 USD per adult and can be booked on viator here: *https://bit.ly/3vBb27v*

3. *Oslo Alternative Culture and Street Food Tour:* Embark on an immersive walking tour to uncover Oslo's alternative facets, accompanied by a delectable exploration of the city's top street food delights. Meeting your guide in the Vulkan neighborhood in the afternoon, ensure you arrive with an appetite as you delve into a culinary journey featuring traditional Norwegian hot dogs, waffles, hot cocoa, and cured meats. In addition to satisfying your taste buds, absorb insights into the city's creative and cultural offerings, enriched by insider stories from your guide. Venture beyond the usual tourist paths to discover the alternative charm of Oslo, accompanied by a generous selection of bites and snacks. Follow your guide to the trendy neighborhoods frequented by locals, and take advantage of exploring on foot to fully absorb the vibrant ambiance of the city. All these enriching experiences are included in the tour. This tour starts from $79 USD per adult and can be booked on viator here: *https://bit.ly/48ykFSL*

4. Oslo Highlights Bike Tour: Hop on a bike for a tour of the city, visiting popular sights and attractions along the way. Experience Oslo in a dynamic and engaging manner, covering more ground than a pedestrian tour. An excellent choice for those who prefer a personalized pace and wish to combine sightseeing with physical activity. This tour starts from $47 USD per adult and can be booked on viator here: **_https://bit.ly/4aYwinF_**

5. 2-Hour Oslo Fjord Sightseeing Cruise: Embark on a serene cruise around the Oslo Fjord, soaking in breathtaking views of the city and its surroundings. Unwind and appreciate the scenery while gaining insights into the city's history and culture through onboard commentary. An ideal option for those seeking a tranquil and picturesque introduction to Oslo. This tour starts from $45 USD per adult and can be booked on viator here: **_https://bit.ly/3vsqQcs_**

Ultimately, the most suitable tour depends on your interests and preferences. I trust this concise overview will assist you in narrowing down your choices!

OSLO UNIQUE EXPERIENCES

1. SOAK IN THE SUMMER SUN AT THE BEACHES — HUK OR PARADISBUKTA

Trade the hustle of the city for seaside serenity at Huk or Paradisbukta. These secluded havens, caressed by emerald waters and sandy shores, offer a sun-drenched escape. Envision basking in the warmth, lulled by the soothing rhythm of waves – a pure summer idyll in Oslo's coastal embrace.

Getting to Huj or Paradisbukta: Getting to Huk and Paradisbukta from Oslo is convenient via public transportation or taxi. Bus line 30 from Nationaltheatret offers a 31-minute journey to Huk and a 36-minute ride to Paradisbukta at 65-85 NOK. Alternatively, a 15-minute train ride from Oslo Sentralstasjon to Lysaker station from where you an take a short walk to either destination cost 40-60 NOK. Taxis provide a quicker 15-18 minute option at 200-250 NOK, hailable on the street or through an app. | ***GPS Coordinates:*** 59.89627844341503, 10.67585377863238

2. HEAR THE BELLS RING AT OSLO CITY HALL

Immerse yourself in the rhythmic symphony of Oslo City Hall's distinctive bells. With each passing hour, their resonant tolls cascade over the harbor, infusing the air with timeless echoes. Stand by the waterfront, let the musical notes envelop you, and sense the vibrant heartbeat of the city beneath your feet. | ***GPS Coordinates:*** 59.91240531195329, 10.733861696875943

3. SIP AN ESPRESSO AT THE TIM WENDELBOE COFFEE ROASTERY

Enter the aromatic sanctuary of Tim Wendelboe, Oslo's revered coffee roastery. Witness the intricate ballet of hand-picked beans expertly roasted, and awaken your senses with a meticulously crafted espresso. Revel in the nuanced flavors, feel the warmth spread, and become a coffee aficionado, Oslo-style. | ***GPS Coordinates:*** 59.92352142608298, 10.755699796876877

4. SOAK IN THE CHARM OF COLORFUL BERGEN

Escape the city center for a day trip to the enchanting Bergen. Stroll amidst its colorful wooden houses, absorb the lively Bryggen wharf, and relish fresh seafood by the harbor. Bergen's unique blend of history, nature, and maritime charm is bound to captivate you. | ***GPS Coordinates:*** 60.38921498140794,

5.326126967211564

5. CHECK OFF THE MAIN ATTRACTIONS WITH A HOP-ON-HOP-OFF BUS TRIP

Let a hop-on-hop-off bus be your guide through Oslo's tapestry of attractions. From the iconic Opera House to the Viking Ship Museum, tick off the city's highlights at your pace. Alight at your whim, explore, and rejoin for the next chapter – a flexible and convenient way to experience Oslo's wonders.

6. MEET SLITHERY SNAKES AT THE OSLO REPTILE PARK

Reptile Adventure: Brace yourself for a thrilling encounter at the Oslo Reptile Park. Witness slithering snakes, captivating lizards, and majestic crocodiles up close. Delve into their intriguing ecology and challenge your fears in this realm of scales and fangs – an expedition for the intrepid explorer within. | *GPS Coordinates of Oslo Reptile Park:* 59.918284883724624, 10.74319589687646

7. SPEND A DAY EXPLORING SOGNEFJORD

Sognefjord's Majesty: Venture beyond the city limits and immerse yourself in the breathtaking beauty of Sognefjord, Norway's longest and deepest fjord. Cruise through emerald waters, framed by towering mountains, kayak in serene coves, or hike along glacier-carved trails – Sognefjord's grandeur is sure to leave you awe-struck. | *GPS Coordinates of Oslo Reptile Park:*

8. RIDE THE ROLLER COASTERS AT TUSENFRYD

Unleash your inner child at Tusenfryd, Scandinavia's largest amusement park. Conquer gravity-defying roller coasters, let out joyous screams on exhilarating rides, and soak in the festive atmosphere. Tusenfryd guarantees a day of adrenaline-pumping fun for all ages.

9. TAKE A HIKE IN NORDMARKA

Lace up your boots and embark on a rejuvenating hike in Nordmarka, Oslo's expansive woodland paradise. Inhale the crisp air, lose yourself in the lush tapestry of trees, and listen to the symphony of birdsong. Nordmarka is a haven for nature lovers, offering tranquility and scenic beauty just steps from the city.

10. WALK DOWN THE DAMSTREDET & TELTHUSBAKKEN STREETS

Traverse Oslo's cobblestone streets with a leisurely stroll down Damstredet & Telthusbakken. Lined with charming cafes and colorful houses, these quaint streets whisper tales of the city's past. Explore hidden courtyards, uncover local gems, and feel the historic pulse of Oslo beneath your feet.

11. HIT THE SLOPES AT SKIMORE OSLO

Unleash your inner snow enthusiast at Skimore Oslo, a year-round winter haven just moments from the city center. Picture making fresh tracks down snowy slopes with stunning fjord views – an exhilarating adventure for skiers and snowboarders.

12. READ A FEW CHAPTERS AT THE DEICHMAN LIBRARY

Retreat from the urban buzz and immerse yourself in literary serenity at the Deichman Library, an architectural marvel overlooking the Oslo Fjord. Whether you curl up with a good book in the sun-drenched atrium, explore their extensive collection, or attend cultural events, it's a bibliophile's paradise.

13. VISIT THE NORWEGIAN PARLIAMENT

Enter the heart of Norwegian democracy at the Stortinget (Norwegian Parliament). Take a guided tour through the impressive neo-classical building, delve into the country's political system, and witness history in action – a captivating glimpse into Norway's governance.

14. SPEND THE DAY AT SOGNSVANN LAKE

Trade city views for serene landscapes at Sognsvann Lake, a picturesque haven nestled in the Nordmarka forest. Whether you opt for a refreshing swim, rent a paddle boat, or explore surrounding trails, it's a perfect retreat for nature lovers seeking tranquility.

15. PAMPER AND PARTY AT SALT

Experience Oslo's unique fusion of pampering and partying at SALT, a lively waterfront complex. From sweating it out in the floating sauna to indulging in a relaxing massage and dancing with fjord views, it's a one-stop destination for rejuvenation and revelry.

16. LACE ON THE SKATES AT THE SPIKERSUPPA RINK

Lace up your skates and twirl across the Spikersuppa ice rink in the heart of Oslo. Whether you challenge yourself to fancy footwork or simply enjoy the lively atmosphere from a nearby café, it's a quintessential winter experience.

17. GO FISHING!

Embrace the local lifestyle with a fishing adventure in Oslo's surrounding waters. Whether you're a seasoned angler or a curious beginner, casting your line in the crystal-clear fjords offers stunning scenery and a potential dinner catch.

18. GO KAYAKING AROUND THE ISLANDS OF OSLO

Explore Oslo's hidden gems from a different perspective with a kayaking tour around the city's charming islands. Paddle through tranquil coves, discover secluded beaches, and witness the city skyline from a unique vantage point – a refreshing escape into nature.

19. WATCH A PLAY AT THE NATIONALTHEATRET

Immerse yourself in the world of Norwegian drama at the Nationaltheatret, a stunning neo-classical theater dating back to the 19th century. Experience the passion and artistry of local actors, be captivated by a thought-provoking play, and soak in the grand atmosphere of this cultural landmark.

20. INDULGE YOUR GAMER SIDE AT TILT ARCADE BAR

Rediscover the joys of classic arcade games at Tilt Arcade Bar. Unleash your inner child, challenge friends to air hockey, battle it out on retro consoles, or sip cocktails amidst a nostalgic setting – a playful escape for gamers of all ages.

OTHER ATTRACTIONS WORTH SEEING IN OSLO

1. Oslo Cathedral: Enter the hallowed halls of Oslo Cathedral, the city's oldest surviving structure dating back to the 12th century. Admire the intricate stained glass windows, a medieval pulpit, and a finely crafted altarpiece, all contributing to the cathedral's Romanesque grandeur.

2. Eidsvoll Building: Witness the historic site where the Norwegian Constitution was signed in 1814, marking a pivotal moment in the nation's democratic journey. Explore the grand halls of the Eidsvoll Building & delve into the details of Norway's fight for independence.

3. Bogstad Manor: Escape the urban hustle and step back in time at Bogstad Manor, an 18th-century estate providing insights into the lives of affluent Norwegians during the Age of Enlightenment. Wander through the manor house, explore lush gardens, and transport yourself to a bygone era.

4. Akerselva River: Take a leisurely stroll along the Akerselva River, once the industrial lifeline of the city. Experience charming bridges, scenic walks, and a glimpse into Oslo's industrial past, revealing a harmonious blend of history and natural beauty.

5. Tribades Plaque: Uncover a piece of Oslo's LGBTQ+ history at the Tribades Plaque. Dating back to 1995, this bronze plaque commemorates two women convicted of lesbian love in the 19th century, serving as a poignant testament to the city's evolving social landscape and the ongoing fight for LGBTQ+ rights.

6. *Kvadraturen:* Immerse yourself in the historic heart of Oslo in Kvadraturen. Laid out after the Great Fire of 1624, this district boasts cobblestone streets, colorful houses, and iconic landmarks like Oslo Cathedral and the National Theatre.

7. *Oslo City Hall:* Appreciate the architectural splendor of Oslo City Hall, the venue for the prestigious Nobel Peace Prize ceremony. Embark on a guided tour to explore its magnificent interiors, including the main hall adorned with murals depicting Norwegian history.

8. *Popsenteret:* Dive into the history of Norwegian music at Popsenteret, the interactive Norwegian Museum of Popular Music. Explore the evolution of music from traditional folk tunes to contemporary pop and electronic genres, offering a hands-on experience in the vibrant world of Norwegian music.

9. Kunstnernes Hus: Explore emerging and established artists at Kunstnernes Hus. As an artist-run gallery, it hosts temporary exhibitions showcasing various art forms, providing a unique opportunity to immerse yourself in the contemporary art scene and witness cutting-edge artistic expression.

10. The Stenersen Museum: Step into the past at The Stenersen Museum, housed in a charming Art Nouveau villa. Explore the diverse collection of Norwegian artist Rolf Stenersen, a contemporary of Edvard Munch, and gain insights into the artistic dialogue between these prominent figures.

11. Hovedøya Island: Experience the car-free paradise of Hovedøya Island, just off the Oslofjord. Explore hiking trails, discover ancient rune stones, and unwind on secluded beaches, offering a perfect blend of nature and tranquility.

12. Tryvann Forest: Indulge in winter sports at Tryvann Forest, featuring downhill skiing and snowboarding in winter. During the summer, explore hiking trails, mountain biking paths, and scenic chairlift rides, providing year-round outdoor adventures.

CHAPTER 4: WHERE TO STAY IN OSLO

Finding the right accommodation is key to a magical adventure in Oslo. We will go through the diverse lodging landscape and decipher the advantages and disadvantages of each option, helping you choose the perfect fit.

Hostels: **Pros:** Super sociable, budget-friendly (dorm beds around 200 NOK), often centrally located, offer common areas with games and events, perfect for solo travelers or those seeking adventure. |*Cons:* Shared bathrooms and facilities, less privacy, can be noisy, not ideal for those seeking tranquility.

Apartments: *Pros:* Spacious, ideal for longer stays, often have kitchen facilities (saving on dining), more privacy, comfortable and homey vibe. | *Cons:* Airbnb availability might fluctuate, cleaning fees can add up, less interaction with other travelers, some apartments might be outside central areas.

Budget Hotels: *Pros:* Affordable (rooms around 600 NOK), decent amenities (WiFi, TVs), often centrally located, provide basic comfort and convenience. | *Cons:* Smaller rooms, less character, might be located on busy streets, limited interaction with locals.

Mid-Range Hotels: *Pros:* Comfortable rooms, stylish design, some offer unique features like spas or rooftop bars, good balance between cost and quality (around 800-1000 NOK), often well-located. | *Cons:* Not as luxurious as high-end options, might lack specific amenities you desire, not budget-friendly for extended stays.

Boutique Hotels: *Pros:* Unique character, personalized service, intimate atmosphere, often have interesting locations or historical buildings, offer local charm and cultural immersion. | *Cons:* Most expensive option (usually above 1500 NOK), limited room availability, might not have all the amenities of larger hotels.

Budget-Friendly Winner: For most travelers, hostels or apartments offer the best bang for your buck. Hostels are ideal for solo adventurers or those on a tight budget, while apartments provide more space and privacy for longer stays.

UNIQUE ACCOMMODATION GEMS

Camping on Bygdøy Island: Budget-friendly with stunning fjord views. | **Houseboats:** Experience life on the water with unique charm. | **Historic hotels**: Immerse yourself in Oslo's past with opulent settings.

BEST BUDGET FRIENDLY ACCOMODATION TO STAY IN OSLO

1. Thon Hotel Munch offers 180 cozy rooms With 115 double and 33 single rooms, complimentary breakfast, and convenient amenities. With eco-certification, it provides modern comforts at a budget-friendly price. The quiet yet central location appeals to eco-conscious travelers seeking tranquility near Oslo's attractions. | **Address:** Munchs gate 5, 0130 Oslo | **Phone:** 23 21 96 00 | **Email**: munch@thonhotels.no: **Website:** Thon Hotel Munch | **GPS Coordinates:** *59.91719200976018, 10.741808425712025*

2. Thon Hotel Astoria in Oslo's city center features 180 rooms with ensuite facilities, Wi-Fi, and amenities. Despite no on-site parking, nearby garages are offered. Built in 1929, reconstructed in 2009, it combines historic charm with modern comforts. Environmentally certified, it offers 67 doubles, 69 singles, totaling 322 beds. | **Address:** Dronningens gate 21, 0154 Oslo | *Phone: 24 14 55 50* | *Email: astoria@thonhotels.no* | *Website: https://www.thonhotels.com/our-hotels/norway/oslo/thon-hotel-astoria* | *GPS Coordinates: 59.91124855115821, 10.74687236988979*

3. **Anker Hotel**, centrally located in Oslo's Grünerløkka district of Oslo is easily accessible from Oslo S train station. It's an ideal base for exploring the city's trendy areas, parks, and attractions. Situated by the Akerselva river, it provides an 8-kilometer walking path from Bjørvika to Maridalsvannet. Close to concert venues and nightlife hotspots like Torggata and Youngstorget. *Address: Storgata 55, 0182 Oslo* | *Phone: 004722997500* | *Email: booking@anker.oslo.no;* | *Website: https://anker-hotel.no* | *GPS Coordinates: 59.917829918620505, 10.757934296876401*

4. Coch's Pension, located near Royal Palace Park, offers a central location, affordable rates, and three room categories. Some include a kitchenette, while others have shared bathrooms. Non-smoking rooms, most with private baths, require advance booking. Breakfast isn't included, but a breakfast deal is available. The pension is environmentally certified in Green Oslo, featuring a meeting room for 35 persons. ***Address:*** Parkveien 25, 0350 Oslo | ***Phone:*** +47 23 33 24 00 | ***E-mail:*** booking@cochs.no | ***Website:*** *https://www.cochspensjonat.no/en* | ***GPS Coordinates:*** 59.920753029495586, 10.728181183383638

5. Topcamp Bogstad Camping offers a year-round camping site in scenic surroundings, a 15-minute drive or 30-minute bus ride from Oslo's city center. It's Norway's largest campsite with 800 pitches, including 300 for caravans with power and 38 for motorhomes. There are 56 cabins, some winter-sheltered, equipped with TVs. The site features two sanitary facilities, a shared kitchen, beach volleyball, a playground, and just five-minute walk to Bogstadvannet lake. Oslo Winter Park is three kilometers away, with cross-country skiing trails nearby. ***Address:*** Ankerveien 117, 0766 Oslo | ***Phone:*** +47 22 51 08 00 | ***Email:*** bogstad@topcamp.no | **Website:** *https:// topcamp.no/en/topcamp-bogstad* | ***GPS Coordinates:*** 59.96264225038627, 10.64228452725038

6. Topcamp Ekeberg Oslo, opens every summer from May 15 to August 19, offers a serene stay with a panoramic view of Oslo's landmarks. Easily accessible to the city center by frequent buses, it accommodates motorhomes, caravans, and tents. The site provides about 600 pitches, with facilities like a reception, showers, a shared kitchen, and a convenience store. Nearby attractions include a petting zoo, horseback riding, a playground, and Ekebergparken Sculpture Park. ***Address:*** Ekebergveien 65, 1181 Oslo | ***Phone:*** +47 22 19 85 68 | ***E-mail:*** ekeberg@topcamp.no | ***Website:*** *https:// topcamp.no/en/topcamp-ekeberg* | **GPS Coordinates:** 59.89842027813216, 10.773522510367817

7. Haraldsheim Youth Hostel, just 4 km from Oslo's center, offers picturesque views of the city and Oslo Fjord. With 88 rooms totaling 315 beds, including ensuite options, it accommodates various group sizes. Guests access a shared kitchen, living room, and a breakfast buffet. Sheets and towels can be rented at the reception. Sleeping bags not allowed. Free parking for cars and buses available. **Address:** Haraldsheimveien 4, 0409 Oslo | **Phone:** +47 22 22 29 65 | **Email:** oslo.haraldsheim@hihostels.no | **Website:** *https://*

www.haraldsheim.no | **GPS Coordinates:** 59.9411, 10.7885.

8. Citybox Oslo offers simple, affordable rooms five minutes from Oslo Central Station. With 341 guest rooms in single, double, twin, and family sizes, it provides practical amenities, including a bathroom, comfortable bed, desk, and clothes-hanging space. Free WiFi is available, and guests check in/out via automated terminals. The hotel lacks a reception but has a Citybox host. Additional beds are available at an extra cost. A TV lounge, kitchen, and self-service laundry room are in the lobby. Breakfast is at Rent Mel. *Address:* Prinsens gate 6, 0152 Oslo | *Phone:* +47 21 42 04 80 | *E-mail:* oslo@cityboxhotels.com | *Websites:* *https://cityboxhotels.com/hotels/oslo/citybox-oslo)* | *GPS Coordinates:* 59.9104, 10.7473

BEST MID-RANGE ACCOMODATION TO STAY IN OSLO

1. Karl Johan Hotel: Situated on the renowned Karl Johans gate in Oslo, the Karl Johan Hotel, a contemporary 3.5-star establishment, underwent stylish renovations in 2021. Boasting 157 rooms adorned with modern décor, lofty ceilings, and expansive windows, the hotel delivers a top-notch breakfast buffet. While it doesn't offer restaurant or room service, the Karl Johan Hotel exudes a relaxed ambiance with high standards and comfort. Its informal atmosphere, coupled with breathtaking views, innovative interior designs, and proximity to shopping and cultural hubs, makes it a treasure for those seeking attractions. *Address:* Karl Johans gate 33, 0162 Oslo, Norway | *Phone:* +47 23 16 17 00 | *Email:* service@karljohan.no | *Website:* *https:// karljohanhotel.com*

2. The Clarion Hotel Oslo is a sleek mid-range option in Oslo's Bjørvika district, near cultural landmarks including the Opera House and the Munch Museum. The hotel's modern lobby showcases rotating artwork, emphasizing local cultural attractions. With over 250 rooms offering city or fjord views, the hotel features a trendy seafood restaurant, a bar, and a vegan-friendly breakfast buffet. The location is central, near the Oslofjord, the Opera House, and the Munch Museum. The hotel promotes sustainability through Nordic Choice Hotels' WeCare program, avoiding unnecessary plastic and encouraging tap water consumption. *Address:* Dronning Eufemias Gate 15, 0191 Oslo , Norway | *Telephone:* +47 21 95 97 50 | *E-mail:* cl.oslo@strawberry.no | *Website:* *https://www.strawberry.se/hotell/norge/oslo/ clarion-hotel-oslo*

3. Oslo Guldsmeden is an eco-friendly boutique hotel near Aker Brygge waterfront. The Balinese-Scandinavian decor includes rustic-chic rooms with four-poster beds and iMac screens, while suites offer standalone tubs. Guests can enjoy organic breakfasts for a fee and relax in the lobby lounge. The Turkish spa provides saunas (fee-based). The hotel promotes sustainability with energy-efficient appliances, organic linens, and recycling initiatives. Its central location offers proximity to Aker Brygge, museums, and public transportation. Rooms vary in size, and the hotel's eclectic interiors create a unique traveler-friendly atmosphere. ***Address:*** Parkveien 78, 0254 Oslo | ***Tel:*** +47 940 13 091 | ***Email:*** oslo@guldsmedenhotels.com | ***Website:*** *https://guldsmedenhotels.com/oslo-guldsmeden*

4. Hotel Christiania Teater, an upscale boutique with art nouveau charm, boasts a historic 1918 building near Oslo's National Theater. With 102 distinct rooms, the hotel offers hardwood floors, mini-bars, and CO Bigelow bath products. Guests enjoy a complimentary breakfast in the trendy Restaurant Teatro, transitioning to a pizzeria with an extensive wine list later. The bi-level lobby lounge, echoing the property's theatrical past, leads to a 600-seat theater hosting various events. The hotel's central location is ideal for exploring Oslo, including the Aker Brygge waterfront. Sustainability initiatives include reduced plastic use and plans for renewable energy. ***Address:*** STORTINGSGATA 16, 0161 OSLO , NORWAY | ***Tel:*** +47 48012329 | ***Email:*** STAY@CHRISTIANIATEATER.COM | ***Website:*** *https:// christianiateater.com/en*

5. Thon Hotel Opera, a modern 480-room mid-range hotel in Oslo's Bjørvika, is centrally located near the Opera House and Central Station. Renovated rooms feature vibrant decor, mini-fridges, and spacious desks. The lobby offers a trendy lounge and an inclusive breakfast buffet. ***Address:*** Dronning Eufemias gate 4, 0191 Oslo | ***Telephone:*** +47 24 10 30 00 | ***Website:*** *https://www.thonhotels.com/our-hotels/norway/oslo/thon-hotel-opera*

6. Camillas Hus is an intimate boutique hotel near Oslo's Royal Palace, offering seven elegantly decorated rooms. Nestled in a historic mid-19th-century building, the hotel provides a quiet retreat with personalized service, free parking, and a complimentary made-to-order breakfast at the adjacent Park 29 restaurant. Rooms feature tasteful decor, mini-bars, and spacious bathrooms with claw-foot tubs. The hotel's authentic feel and proximity to Palace Park and Frogner add to its charm, while the limited reception hours are supplemented by online availability for guest assistance. ***Address:*** Parkveien 31, 0350 Oslo, Norway | ***Phone:*** + 47 948 560 15 | info@camillashus.no | booking@camillashus.no | ***Website:*** *https://*

NICHOLAS INGRAM

camillashusenglish.squarespace.com

BEST LUXURIOUS ACCOMODATION TO STAY IN OSLO

1. The Thief: Situated on Oslo's Tjuvholmen, The Thief is an audacious design boutique hotel at the water's edge, surrounded by art galleries and trendy establishments. Rooms feature in-built sound systems, private balconies, and Nespresso machines. The hotel offers spa treatments, a Turkish hamam, sauna, and a rooftop terrace with a contemporary Norwegian cuisine restaurant. Guests enjoy free entry to the Astrup Fearnley Museum. The central location allows easy access to Aker Brygge and Oslo's attractions. *__Address:__* Landgangen 1, 0252 Oslo, Norway | *__Phone:__* +47 24 00 40 00 | Email: *stay@thethief.com* | *__Websites:__* *https://thethief.com/en* | *__GPS Coordinates:__* 59.90818769312288, 10.721038384657378

2. Hotel Continental is a centrally located 5-star hotel with 152 rooms in Oslo. Rooms feature amenities, cable TV, and free in-room Internet. Guests have access to a 24-hour gym and a lobby lounge with Edward Munch lithographs. Fine dining is available at Restaurant Eik Annen Etage, and the historic Theatercaféen offers a century-old dining experience. The hotel's maritime-style Steamen Café serves drinks and snacks. The National Theatre is across the street, and the Royal Palace is a 5-minute walk away. *__Address:__* Stortingsgata 24/26, 0117 Oslo, Norway | *__Phone:__* +47 22 82 40 00 | *__Email:__* booking@hotelcontinental.no | *__Website:__* *https://www.hotelcontinental.no/eng* | *__GPS Coordinates:__* 59.914686672382736, 10.733514199320817

3. Hotel Bristol, is an elegant hotel in Oslo's city center with 240 rooms. Centrally located, it offers proximity to shopping, Karl Johans gate, the Royal Palace, museums, and Aker Brygge waterfront. Since 1920, the hotel has exuded tradition, quality, and service. The rooms feature antique-style furniture, and guests enjoy free Wi-Fi, gym, and sauna access. The Bristol Grill offers traditional Norwegian cuisine, and the Library Bar, a historical meeting place, features live piano music. The hotel is only a 3-minute walk from the National Theatre and the National Gallery. *__Address:__* Kristian IVs gate 7, 0164 Oslo, Norway | *__Phone:__* +47 22 82 60 00 | *__Email:__* post@bristol.no

| *Websites: https://hotelbristol.no/en* | *GPS Coordinates:* 59.9158272416888, 10.739285769314757

4. Lysebu Hotel, rated 8.9, is situated atop Tryvannshøyden Hill in Oslo. With 84 rooms, it offers free WiFi and parking, along with panoramic views. The in-house restaurant serves Norwegian cuisine, and guests can enjoy a 5-course weekly menu with wine pairings. The hotel features a wine cellar, art exhibitions, live music, a large garden, an indoor pool, and a fireplace lounge. Activities include skiing, hiking, and cycling, with Oslo city center accessible via a 40-minute metro ride. *Address:* Lysebuveien 12, 0790 Oslo, Norway | *Phone:* +47 21 51 10 00 | *Email:* resepsjon@lysebu.no | *Website: https:// lysebu.no/en* | *GPS Coordinates*: 59.97836221690635, 10.6558284

5. Grand Hotel Oslo, established in 1874 with 233 rooms, is a prestigious luxury hotel hosting Norway's people, international guests, world leaders, celebrities, and Nobel laureates. Guests under 18 must be with a parent or guardian. The Eight Roof Top Bar and Artesia Spa have specific operational hours and policies.
Address: Karl Johans gate. 31, 0159 Oslo, Norway | *Phone:* +47 23 21 20 00 | *Email:* grand@grand.no | *Website: https://grand.no/en* | *GPS Coordinates:* 59.9142723925657, 10.7394509

6. Thon Hotel Rozenkrantz Oslo, with 151 rooms and a four-star rating, offers eco-friendly accommodations near Aker Brygge and Oslo Central Station. Renovated and equipped with amenities like free WiFi, the hotel features a restaurant, bar, lounge, fitness center, and convenient proximity to Oslo's attractions and transportation hubs. *Address:* Rosenkrantz' gate 1, 0159 Oslo, Norway | *Phone:* +47 23 31 55 00 | *Website: https:// www.thonhotels.com/our-hotels/norway/oslo/thon-hotel-rosenkrantz-oslo* | *GPS Coordinates:* 59.9157269366483, 10.740598614068432

7. Losby Gods Manor, a historical 4-star estate with 9 rooms provides stylish accommodation in a picturesque setting, just 20 minutes from Oslo and 30 minutes from Gardermoen Airport. You can enjoy spacious en-suite rooms, an in-house restaurant, private wine cellar, golf courses, hiking trails, and complimentary amenities. ***Address:*** Losby Gods AS, Losbyveien 270, 1475 Finstadjordet | ***Phone:*** +47 67 92 33 00 | ***Email:*** reservations@losbygods.no | ***Website:*** *https://www.losbygods.no/english* | ***GPS Coordinates:*** 59.88728444528894, 10.9829444

CHAPTER 5:
SAVORING
NORWEGIAN CUISINE

WHAT TO EAT IN OSLO

Norwegian cuisine is shaped by a harsh landscape, the reliance on fish, game, and hardy grains. Abundant seafood from the coastline and preservation techniques like drying and smoking contribute to traditional dishes. Pickling and fermentation add tangy flavors, while global influences from Viking voyages and neighboring countries introduce spices and ingredients like rice. The "New Nordic" cuisine, led by chefs championing sustainability, brings a modern twist to traditional recipes with a focus on fresh, local ingredients. Notable restaurants like Maaemo in Oslo have gained international acclaim, showcasing Norway's culinary excellence. Norwegian cuisine is not just about food; it's a tale of resilience, resourcefulness, and a profound connection to nature. For a unique culinary adventure, explore the vibrant flavors and innovative spirit of modern Norwegian gastronomy, and don't miss trying *aquavit*, a traditional spirit often paired with seafood dishes. Here are some top foods you shouldn't miss while in Oslo:

BRUNOST: This caramelized brown cheese is not for the faint-hearted, boasting an intense, nutty sweetness that tantalizes the taste buds. It serves as a perfect complement to crusty bread or succulent berries. | ***FISKEKAKE:*** Beyond being mere hushpuppies, these fish cakes boast a crispy exterior and a fluffy interior. Picture chunks of cod and salmon infused with dill and lemon, encased in a golden panko crust, inviting a dip in creamy aioli. | ***FÅRIKÅL:*** A winter comfort dish, fårikål features tender mutton surrounded by sweet, caramelized cabbage, emitting an aroma reminiscent of autumn leaves and cozy hearths. Boiled potatoes act as the ideal canvas for soaking up the rich gravy. | ***SMØRBRØD:*** Going beyond a typical sandwich, these open-faced delicacies serve as culinary canvases. Whether it's smoked salmon with tangy dill creme fraiche on dark rye or layers of roast beef, horseradish, and beetroot, they offer a savory explosion of flavors. | ***KOMLE:*** These unassuming potato flatbreads transcend mere filler, presenting fluffy rounds with slightly crisp edges, ready to be adorned with butter, jam, or savory toppings like cured meats and cheese. | ***RAKFISK:*** Despite its initial intimidating sound, this fermented trout is a revelation for the adventurous palate. The months-long fermentation process yields an intense, umami-rich flavor that is surprisingly delicate and addictively delicious. | ***KRANSEKAKE***: More than a dessert, this towering almond ring cake serves as a centerpiece. Imagine delicate almond cookies stacked into a precarious tower with meringue, punctuated by occasional nuggets of candied fruit. | ***RØKT LAKS (SMOKED SALMON)***, a traditional Norwegian dish widely enjoyed globally and often likened to bacon, is prepared by smoking salmon with wood chips for several hours until it attains a deep, rich brown color, imparting a smoky and salty flavor. Typically served as an appetizer or snack, it also finds its way into sandwiches, salads, or various dishes, offering a good supply of protein and omega-3 fatty acids. | ***KJØTTKAKER***, or meatballs, constitute another popular Norwegian fare, crafted from ground beef, breadcrumbs, onions, and spices. Often accompanied by a brown sauce or gravy, they can be enjoyed as a main course or side dish, providing a rich source of protein and iron. | ***LEFSE***, a thin flatbread made from potatoes, flour, and water, is commonly served with butter, cheese, or jam. It doubles as a versatile ingredient for wraps or sandwiches and is a wholesome source of carbohydrates and fiber. | ***MALAHOVE***, a robust dish featuring sheep's head, involves boiling the head, removing the meat, and cooking it in a flavorful sauce. Typically served with potatoes, carrots, and onions, Malahove is a hearty winter meal known for tender and flavorful sheep's head meat, offering a robust source of protein and iron. | ***UTEFISK***, a catch-of-the-day dish prevalent in Norwegian restaurants, primarily consists of fresh seafood, often fish caught on the same day. Paired with boiled potatoes, vegetables, and a sauce, Utefisk allows the enjoyment of locally sourced seafood, with the specific type varying based on season and region. It serves as a nutritious source of protein and omega-3 fatty acids. | ***NORWEGIAN SALMON***: Oslo, known for its exceptional salmon, presents this delectable fish in various preparations. Enjoy it smoked on rye bread with a dollop of dill mustard, or treat yourself to an extravagant multi-course seafood feast. | ***FRESH PRAWNS:*** Delight in a plate of juicy prawns directly from the Oslofjord, available in boiled, grilled, or fried options. Ideal for a light lunch or as a shared appetizer. | ***OSLO'S FISH AND CHIPS***: The city puts a unique spin on the classic British dish. Anticipate a serving of fresh, flaky fish enveloped in a light, crispy batter, accompanied by chunky fries and homemade tartar sauce. | ***WAFFLES:*** The Norwegians have a profound appreciation for waffles, and Oslo is no different. Indulge in these light and warm delights adorned with a variety of toppings, ranging from traditional

OSLO TRAVEL GUIDE

brown cheese and sour cream to fresh berries and whipped cream. |
CINNAMON TWIRLS (KANELSNURRER): These cinnamon rolls are the perfect on-the-go sweet treat. Soft, doughy, and filled with a burst of cinnamon flavor, they provide a delightful way to satisfy your sugar cravings. |
CHOCOLATE (SJOKOLADE): Norway boasts some of the finest chocolates globally. Choose from handmade truffles, decadent marzipan bars, or velvety milk chocolate with a variety of flavors.

RESTAURANTS & MUST-TRY DISHES

To have the ultimate culinary experience in Oslo, here is a curated list of must-visit restaurants in the city. It contains renowned Michelin-starred, mid-range and budget-friendly restaurants. Our selection mirrors the diverse gastronomic scene of Oslo. Beyond just the ambiance, we've spotlighted signature dishes that are absolute must-tries.

BUDGET-FRIENDLY

1. Happolati: A lively hotspot embracing global street food, Happolati offers a variety of tapas-style dishes from around the world. Share small plates and soak in the vibrant atmosphere. | *Recommended Dishes:* Try Korean pancakes (kimchijeon), Moroccan lamb skewers (brochettes), and Spanish chorizo and peppers (pimientos de padron). | *Location:* ST. OLAVS PLASS 2 , 0165 OSLO | *Website:* *https://www.happolati.no* | *Getting there:* Close to T-bane stop Tøyen or tram stops like Olaf Ryes plass or Folketeateret.

2. Katla: Experience traditional Icelandic cuisine with a modern twist at Katla, a cozy hidden gem. The warm and inviting atmosphere makes Katla an ideal spot for a casual yet memorable dining experience. Enjoy a modern take on traditional Icelandic comfort food in a cozy hidden setting. | *Recommended Dishes:* Lamb kofta in yogurt sauce, pan-fried cod with crispy potatoes and pickled beets, or the classic skyr cake with berries. | *Website:* *https:// www.katlaoslo.no/english* | i Universitetsgata 12, 0164 Oslo

3. Skaal Matbar: This small and lively bar infuses Nordic flavors into playful tapas-style dishes. Share plates, sip cocktails, and immerse yourself in the energetic atmosphere. | *Recommended Dishes:* Try the cured reindeer carpaccio with pickled blueberries, crispy pork belly bao buns, or their signature creamy cod roe toast.
Location: Olaf Ryes Plass 12, Oslo | *Website:* *https://www.skaalmatbar.no* | *Access:* Conveniently located near T-bane stop Tøyen or tram stops like Olaf Ryes plass or Folketeateret.

4. Haralds Vaffel: A staple since the 1930s, Haralds Vaffel is Oslo's renowned waffle stand, known for its crispy, golden waffles. Embark on a topping adventure, choosing from classic brown cheese and jam to more adventurous options like shrimp or caviar. | **_Recommended Dishes:_** Try the "Brunost og syltetøy" (brown cheese and jam) for a traditional experience, or opt for the "Brunost og bacon" for a savory twist. Top it off with a scoop of vanilla ice cream! | **_Location:_** Olaf Ryes plass 3, 0552 Oslo | **_Website:_** _https:// www.haraldsvaffel.no_ | **_Access:_** it's a pleasant 15-minute walk from Tøyen Park or Grünerløkka

5. Mamma Pizza Osteria: Bringing the lively spirit of Italian dining to Oslo, Mamma Pizza Osteria is a bustling osteria offering wood-fired pizzas teeming with fresh ingredients, handmade pastas, and a vibrant atmosphere. | **_Recommended Dishes:_** Indulge in the "Tartufo" pizza with mozzarella, black truffle, and parmesan, or opt for the comforting "Gnocchi al pesto" for your pasta fix. Conclude your meal with a shared tiramisu for dessert! | **_Location:_** Dronningens gate 22, 0154 Oslo | Russeløkkveien 26, 0251 Oslo | **_Website:_** _https://www.mammapizza.no_ | **_Access:_** To get to the outlet at Dronningens gate, its a 15 minutes from Karl Johans gate or the Nationaltheatret station | To get to the outlet at Russelokkveien Take the metro line 3 (Fjordbo) to Frøen station. From there, it's a roughly 5-minute walk to Russeløkkveien 26, a pleasant 30-minute stroll from Frognerparken, 20-minute walk from Majorstuen or Vika

6. Baker Hansen: Baker Hansen is a local chain restaurants with over 20 outlets in Oslo and offers fresh pastries, breads, and sandwiches at very reasonable prices. Grab a cinnamon bun and a latte for under 50 NOK – perfect for a quick bite. **_Address:_** 1361 Østerås | **_Telephone:_** (+47) 94 00 12 60 | **_E-mail:_** post@bakerhansen.no | **_Website:_** https://www.bakerhansen.no

MID-RANGE

1. The Vandelay: Enjoy a creative Norwegian take on American comfort food in a laid-back, hipster-cool atmosphere which makes it the perfect spot for a satisfying and relaxed meal. | **_Recommended Dishes_**: Juicy burger with local cheese, mac and cheese with brown cheese, or the adventurous reindeer Reuben. | **_Address:_** Operagata 30, 0194 Oslo, Norway | **_Phone:_** +47 40

63 14 11 | *Website:* *https://restaurantguru.com/The-Vandelay-Oslo/menu* | GPS Coordinates 59.90706715316044, 10.757743370488331

2. Savage: Indulge your wild side at Savage, a wood-fired grill restaurant celebrating robust flavors and rustic cooking. Revel in wood-fired meats and bold flavors in this industrial-chic grill haven. | **Recommended Dishes**: Any cut of meat from the wood-fired grill, charred vegetables, and the luscious bone marrow. | **Address:** Nedre Slottsgate 2, 0153 Oslo, Norway | **Phone:** +47 92 29 18 40 | **Website:** *https://www.restaurantsavage.no* | *GPS Coordinate:* 59.90967088722154, 10.740231713493031

3. Kafeteria August: Positioned centrally, this restaurant celebrates the goodness of fresh, seasonal ingredients in a laid-back ambiance. Expect a menu featuring vibrant salads, hearty stews, and impeccably grilled seafood. | **Recommended Dishes:** Explore the lunch menu with daily specials or opt for the Kjøkkenfest (dinner feast) for a shared culinary experience. | **Location:** Universitetsgata 9, 0164 Oslo | **Website:** *https://kafeteriaaugust.no* | **GPS Coordinates:** 59.9171, 10.7385

4. Arakataka: A stylish vegan restaurant celebrating plant-based cuisine with creativity and flair. Expect artfully presented dishes bursting with flavors. | **Recommended Dishes:** Dive into the ever-changing "Green Feast" menu or savor the beetroot tartare with cashew "cheese." | **Location:** Mariboes gate 7B, 0183 Oslo, Norway | **Website:** *https://www.arakataka.no* | **GPS Coordinates:** 59.9165, 10.7506

5. Smalhans: Embracing Copenhagen's smørrebrød tradition, this historic restaurant in Oslo offers open-faced sandwiches with delightful toppings. Enjoy traditional classics and inventive modern variations. | **Recommended Dishes:** Savor smørrebrød with classic combinations like roast beef and remoulade or herring and onion rings, or explore their creative seasonal options. | **Location**: Ullevålsveien 43, 0171 Oslo, Norway | **Website:** *https://smalhans.no* | **GPS Coordinates:** 59.9239, 10.7398

6. Schlägergården: Transport yourself back in time at this traditional

Norwegian restaurant housed in a historic building. Feast on hearty, comforting dishes such as stews, roast meats, and fresh fish.

| *Recommended Dishes:* Indulge in fårikål (steamed cabbage and mutton), pinnekjøtt (cured lamb ribs), or their signature potato dumplings with brown butter and lingonberries. | *Location:* Lilleakerveien 30, 0283 Oslo, Norway | *Website:* https://www.schlagergarden.no | *GPS Coordinates:* 59.9204, 10.6353

MICHELIN STARRED

1. Maaemo: Experience molecular gastronomy meets Nordic bounty in an intimate setting. | *Restaurant Category*: Michelin (Three Stars) | *Recommended Dishes:* Seasonal Norwegian tasting menu with highlights like reindeer tartare and langoustine in seawater. | *Address:* Dronning Eufemias gate 23, 0194 Oslo, Norway | *Website: http://www.maaemo.no* | *GPS coordinates*: 59.9077, 10.7582

2. Vaaghals: Seafood enthusiasts should not miss Vaaghals, a Michelin-starred gem committed to sustainability and innovation putting sustainable seafood in the spotlight. | *Restaurant Category:* Michelin (One Star) | *Recommended Dishes*: Turbot with Jerusalem artichoke puree and truffle, monkfish in seaweed butter, or the ever-changing crudo selection. | *Address*: Dronning Eufemias gate 8, 0191 Oslo, Norway | *Website: http://www.vaaghals.com* | *GPS coordinates*: 59.9085, 10.7567

3. Mon Oncle: This Michelin-starred establishment seamlessly merges French culinary techniques with local Nordic ingredients, presenting an elegant and contemporary dining experience. | *Type of Restaurant:* Michelin (One Star) | *Recommended Dishes:* Indulge in the tasting menu that highlights seasonal flavors or try the signature roasted pigeon with cherry sauce. | *Location:* Universitetsgata 9, 0164 Oslo, Norway | *Website: https://mononcle.no* | *GPS coordinates*: 59.91749, 10.73899

4. Kontrast: An intimate eatery championing locally sourced ingredients and minimalist plates, emphasizing pure flavor and texture. | *Type of Restaurant:* Michelin (One Star) | *Recommended Dishes:* Explore the tasting menu showcasing contemporary Nordic cuisine or savor the signature langoustine tartar with caviar and dill. | ***Location:*** Maridalsveien 15a, 0175 Oslo, Norway | ***Website:*** *https://www.restaurant-kontrast.no* | ***Access:*** Accessible by ferry from Aker Brygge or bus 33 from Rådhusplassen. | ***GPS coordinates***: 59.92344, 10.75103

5. Hot Shop: Formerly a sex shop, this Michelin-starred bistro now serves contemporary seasonal dishes with a playful twist. Anticipate lively, elegant plates and a vibrant atmosphere. | ***Type of Restaurant***: Michelin (One Star) | ***Recommended Dishes:*** Opt for the surprise tasting menu featuring the day's freshest ingredients or indulge in the signature roast duck with cherries and fennel. | ***Location:*** Københavngata 18, 0566 Oslo | ***Website:*** *https:// www.restauranthotshop.no* | ***Phone***: +4746673718| ***GPS coordinates***: 59.92831, 10.76856

6. Hedone: This elegant restaurant combines French gastronomy with a contemporary Nordic twist, presenting beautifully crafted dishes with stunning flavor combinations. | ***Recommended Dishes:*** Delight in the tasting menu showcasing seasonal Norwegian ingredients or savor the signature pigeon roasted with beetroot and juniper. | ***Location:*** Skovveien 15, 0257 Oslo, Norway | ***Website:*** *https://www.hedone.no* | ***Phone:*** +4722120502 | ***GPS coordinates***: 59.91797, 10.71845

COOKING CLASSES

1. iLupen: *Emphasis:* Contemporary Norwegian and international cuisine, highlighting seasonal ingredients. | *Experience:* Intimate, hands-on sessions conducted in a professional kitchen. Gain insights from skilled chefs and partake in a communal meal afterward. | *Ideal for:* Aspiring home chefs seeking top-notch guidance and innovative culinary creations. | **Website:** *https://www.ilupen.no*

2. Thai Matkurs Norge: *Emphasis:* Authentic Thai cooking methods and recipes using fresh, locally-sourced ingredients. | ***Experience:*** Energetic and participatory classes led by experienced Thai instructors. Master the art of fragrant curries, stir-fries, and delightful desserts. | ***Ideal for:*** Culinary enthusiasts looking to deepen their understanding of Thai culinary traditions. | **Website:** *https://thaicookingoslo.weebly.com* | Price: Classes start from $79 USD

3. Nordisk Experiences: Emphasis: Traditional Nordic dishes and food culture, often infused with historical elements. | ***Experience:*** Unique sessions incorporating foraging, open-air cooking, and storytelling. Immerse yourself in the culinary heritage of the region. | ***Ideal for:*** Adventurous food lovers keen on exploring Nordic gastronomy beyond contemporary interpretations. | **Website:** *http://www.nordisk-experiences.no* | ***Phone***: +4791393198 | ***Email:*** contact@nordisk-experiences.no

4. Oslo Lapper: *Emphasis:* Enjoyable and relaxed workshops centered on crafting traditional Norwegian "lapper" (flatbreads). | ***Experience:*** Family-friendly atmosphere featuring interactive baking and storytelling. Learn about local food traditions while savoring freshly baked flatbreads. | *Ideal for:* Groups seeking a laid-back and interactive experience with a touch of Norwegian culture. | ***Email:*** *oslolapper@gmail.com*

5. Tumulus Grove: *Emphasis:* Wood-fired cooking and foraging experiences set in a picturesque natural environment. | ***Experience:*** Acquire skills in open-fire cooking using foraged ingredients and traditional methods.

Connect with nature for a rustic culinary adventure. | ***Ideal for:*** Nature enthusiasts and culinary aficionados desiring a distinctive and immersive outdoor cooking experience. | ***Website:*** *http://www.tumulusgrove.com* | ***Email:*** contact@nordisk-experiences.no | ***Phone:*** +4793400191

Note: This information is derived from publicly available sources and may not cover all details. For specific information and schedules, it is recommended to visit individual cooking class websites.

STREET FOOD SPOTS

1. *Oslo Street Food:* Situated in the vibrant Tjuvholmen neighborhood, Oslo Street Food is a bustling hub offering a global smorgasbord. With lively vibes and colorful food trucks, it's a perfect spot for adventurous foodies. | ***Address:*** Tjuvholmen, Oslo. | ***Directions:*** Several buses stop near Tjuvholmen, including lines 81, 33, and 28.

2. *Barcode Street Food:* Located in the trendy Barcode district, Barcode Street Food is a modern market filled with gourmet eateries and pop-up food stalls. It's ideal for a stylish and delicious lunch break. | ***Address:*** Dronning Eufemias gate 8, Oslo. | ***Directions:*** Buses 300, 390, and 200 all stop near Barcode.

3. *Grønland Food Market:* Immerse yourself in Oslo's multicultural melting pot at Grønland Food Market, offering a kaleidoscope of flavors from around the world. | ***Address:*** Grønlandsleiret 35, Oslo. ***Directions:*** Buses 30, 31, and 37 all stop near Grønland.

4. *Mathallen Oslo:* Housed in a charming former industrial building, Mathallen Oslo is a haven for gourmet enthusiasts, offering street-style treats alongside high-end delicacies. | ***Address***: Akersgata 59, Oslo. | ***Directions:*** Train: Take the train to Oslo Sentralstasjon then walk 15 minutes towards the river. | ***Subway:*** Take lines 3, 4, or 5 to Tøyengata then walk 10 minutes. | ***Bus:*** Buses 30, 31, and 37 all stop near Mathallen.

5. *Vippa Food Court:* Perched on Oslo's harborfront, Vippa Food Court in converted shipping containers offers stunning views and a diverse food scene. | ***Address:*** Akershusstranda, Oslo. | ***Directions: Ferry***: Hop on the Akershusstranda ferry from Aker Brygge. | ***Bus***: Bus 82 and 200 stop near Akershusstranda. | ***Walking:*** Take a scenic walk from Aker Brygge along the waterfront (about 15 minutes).

CHAPTER 6: OSLO FESTIVAL AND NIGHTLIFE THRILL

OSLO FESTIVAL

Oslo boasts a vibrant festival scene throughout the year, showcasing a diverse array of cultural, musical, and artistic expressions. These festivals contribute to the city's dynamic atmosphere, drawing both locals and visitors into the celebration of various forms of creativity. From music and film to literature and multicultural events, these festivals offer a platform for emerging talents and established artists alike. The festival calendar typically spans different seasons, allowing residents and tourists to immerse themselves in a rich tapestry of experiences. Whether it's the exploration of avant-garde compositions, the joyous celebration of diverse cultures, or the appreciation of cinematic arts, Oslo's festivals collectively contribute to the city's cultural tapestry, making it an exciting destination for those seeking an immersive and enriching experience.

Warm weather ushers in open-air music festivals, where lively beats and soaring vocals resonate. Imagine sun-kissed crowds swaying to indie rock on grassy hillsides or passionately headbanging to intense metal amidst historic remnants. Immerse yourself in specialized festivals devoted to jazz, chamber music, or the diverse rhythms of world music. These gatherings spotlight musical expertise and introduce audiences to hidden treasures from various corners of the world.

Experience a spiritual atmosphere at the International Church Music Festival, blending sacred voices and ancient instruments for a transcendent encounter. Miniøya, a dedicated children's festival, promises joy with engaging workshops, lively performances, and interactive activities sparking young imaginations.

MUST-WITNESS ANNUAL FESTIVALS

1. Oslo Jazz Festival (August): Immerse yourself in a captivating week-long celebration of jazz, featuring over 70 concerts in various venues. From traditional swing to avant-garde performances, the festival caters to both jazz enthusiasts and those new to the genre.Witness Oslo's vibrant jazz scene, from legends like Jan Garbarek to emerging talents in intimate club settings. Appreciate the genre's evolution while soaking in the city's summery ambiance.

2. Øya Festival (August): An open-air celebration of rock, pop, and indie music on Midtøyra island, featuring international headliners and local talents across multiple stages. Enjoy live performances by favorite bands in a scenic setting. Discover new global acts amidst vibrant stalls, food trucks, and an inclusive festival atmosphere.

3. Holmenkollen Ski Festival (March): Experience the excitement of one of the world's most iconic ski jumps, featuring thrilling competitions in ski jumping and cross-country skiing. | Immerse yourself in the electrifying atmosphere as elite athletes compete against the backdrop of Oslo's stunning winter scenery. Gain insight into Norwegian traditions and sporting prowess.

4. Oslo International Church Music Festival (June): Transforming Oslo's churches into concert halls, this festival celebrates the fusion of sacred spaces and music, offering a diverse program of classical music, choral performances, and organ recitals. | Discover musical treasures within architectural marvels, spanning ancient Gregorian chants to contemporary compositions. Immerse yourself in the tranquil ambiance of consecrated spaces.

5. Oslo Food Festival (September): Embark on a culinary journey through local and international flavors, featuring renowned chefs, gourmet foods, and street vendors. | Indulge in delectable bites from top restaurants and emerging talents. Explore the diversity of Scandinavian and international cuisine through cooking demonstrations, workshops, and talks by celebrated chefs.

6. Pride Parade and Festival (June): Celebrate love, inclusivity, and LGBTQ + rights with Oslo's vibrant Pride Parade and Festival, featuring flamboyant costumes, live music, and a joyous celebration of diversity. | Witness the city come alive with acceptance and unity. Experience the positive energy and support the fight for LGBTQ+ rights at this vibrant festival.

7. Inferno Metal Festival (March): Dive into the darker side of music with international and Norwegian black metal, doom, and heavy rock bands creating an intense and exhilarating atmosphere. | Explore the raw energy and creativity of the metal scene with a diverse lineup and immersive stage shows. Brace yourself for a bold and adventurous sonic experience.

8. By:Larm (March): Discover the future of music at By:Larm, showcasing up-and-coming Nordic and international acts across various genres. |Be among the first to witness emerging talent before they hit the mainstream. Dive into a diverse soundscape, exploring new genres and contributing to the future of music.

9. OverOslo (August): Soar above the city and embrace the summer vibes at OverOslo! This elevated festival turns rooftops throughout Oslo into al fresco stages, featuring music, DJs, culinary delights, and awe-inspiring vistas. | Immerse yourself in Oslo from a distinct vantage point. Delight in expansive cityscapes illuminated by the warm hues of the summer sun. Move to the rhythm of diverse beats curated by skilled DJs beneath the starlit sky. Indulge in delectable treats from local vendors while mingling with fellow festival enthusiasts amidst the city's elevated landscapes. OverOslo promises a lively, personal ambiance that sets it apart from any other festival experience.

10. Findings Festival (March): Dive into the future at this forward-looking festival. Anticipate talks, workshops, and exhibitions delving into technology, music, and innovation, featuring everything from AI art installations to live coding performances. | Draw inspiration from cutting-edge ideas and interact with the pioneering minds of tomorrow. Connect with creative professionals, explore emerging trends, and witness the fusion of art, technology, and futuristic thinking.

of string quartets, woodwind quintets, and other unique chamber music combinations.

OSLO NIGHTLIFE

Oslo boasts a diverse array of nighttime activities, ranging from chic bars and nightclubs to vibrant live music venues and cultural happenings. Here's an overview of Oslo's nocturnal offerings:

Bars and Pubs: Oslo showcases a multitude of bars & pubs, each catering to unique preferences. Districts like Grünerløkka & Aker Brygge are renowned for their lively concentrations of bars, fostering a dynamic atmosphere. The surge in popularity of microbreweries & craft beer bars has introduced an array of local and international brews to the scene. | ***Nightclubs:*** Oslo boasts diverse nightclubs with unique themes and music genres, ranging from EDM to versatile playlists of pop, hip-hop, and alternative tunes. The city's nightclub scene constantly evolves, with the popularity of venues shifting over time, adding dynamism to the nightlife. | ***Live Music:*** Oslo pulsates with a vibrant live music scene, offering venues that span genres, from rock & jazz to indie and electronic. Whether in concert halls or intimate spaces, the city regularly hosts performances by both local and international artists. | ***Cultural Events:*** The city plays host to a myriad of cultural events, encompassing art exhibitions, theater performances, and film screenings, enriching the nightlife experience for those with a penchant for the arts. | ***Restaurants & Cafés:*** Some restaurants & cafés in Oslo extend their operating hours into the evening, providing a quieter, more relaxed nightlife option. This caters to those seeking a serene atmosphere amidst the bustling city. | ***Seasonal Variations:*** Oslo's nightlife shifts with the seasons, with summer featuring outdoor events & festivals, and winter bringing more indoor activities. This seasonal variation adds dynamism to the city's nighttime scene.

TOP CHOICE NIGHTLIFE VENUES

Oslo's nocturnal landscape mirrors the richness and diversity of its culture. From intimate coffee retreats to lively cocktail hubs, the city caters to a wide array of preferences after sunset. Here's a glimpse into 6 top choice destinations, each boasting its distinctive allure:

1. TIM WENDELBOE: A haven for coffee enthusiasts, Tim Wendelboe stands out as a micro-roastery and café, dedicated to serving impeccably sourced beans roasted to perfection. | ***WHY IT IS WORTH VISITING:*** What makes it noteworthy: Dive into the world of specialty coffee with precisely brewed single-origin beans and innovative brewing techniques. The minimalist, well-lit space emanates a distinct Scandinavian charm, complemented by baristas eager to share their profound coffee knowledge. | ***WEBSITE:*** *https:// timwendelboe.no*

2. FUGLEN: Fuglen transcends the typical bar experience, offering a sensory journey. Concealed behind an unmarked door, this intimate speakeasy transports patrons to the golden age of cocktails with its vintage decor and expertly crafted drinks. | ***WHY IT IS WORTH VISITING:*** Immerse yourself in the speakeasy ambiance and allow skilled mixologists to surprise you with inventive cocktails. The menu evolves with the seasons, showcasing unique flavor fusions and locally sourced ingredients. Expect a wait, as Fuglen's exclusivity adds to its allure. | ***WEBSITE:*** *https://fuglen.no/Fuglen-Oslo-Sentrum*

3. TERRITORIET: A haven for wine enthusiasts, Territoriet boasts an extensive wine list featuring hundreds of options by the glass, ideal for exploring new varietals and vintages. | ***WHY IT IS WORTH VISITING:*** Whether you're a seasoned wine connoisseur or a curious beginner, Territoriet's knowledgeable staff is ready to guide you through their impressive selection. Indulge in your chosen wines alongside delectable small plates, all within a lively yet sophisticated atmosphere. | ***WEBSITE:*** *https://www.territoriet.no/* english

4. TORGGATA BOTANISKE: Step out of the urban hustle into Torggata Botaniske, a lush bar adorned with greenery and an on-site herb garden. | ***WHY IT IS WORTH VISITING:*** Enjoy botanical cocktails infused with fresh herbs and spices, surrounded by vibrant plants and twinkling fairy lights. The cozy ambiance and imaginative drinks make Torggata Botaniske a distinctive and revitalizing choice for a night out. | **WEBSITE:** *https:// www.torggatabotaniske.no*

5. KULTURHUSET: Beyond a mere nightlife venue, Kulturhuset serves as a cultural nexus hosting concerts, exhibitions, theater performances, and club nights. | **WHY IT IS WORTH VISITING:** Experience a live music show, dance to the beats of a DJ set, or soak in the creative energy of this multifaceted venue. With a diverse program offering something every night, Kulturhuset stands as a dynamic melting pot of Oslo's artistic scene. | **WEBSITE:** *https:// www.kulturhusetioslo.no*

6. ROULEURS OF OSLO: Unleash your inner dancer at Rouleurs of Oslo, a vintage roller disco adorned with neon lights, funky tunes, and a retro atmosphere. | **WHY IT IS WORTH VISITING:** Lace up your roller skates and get ready to groove! Rouleurs promises a fun and nostalgic night out, featuring themed DJ sets, dance lessons, and a healthy dose of 70s and 80s kitsch. It's the perfect setting to let loose and flaunt your moves in a carefree environment. | **WEBSITE:** *https://www.rouleuroslo.no*

CHAPTER 7: BEYOND OSLO - DAY TRIPS & NEARBY ADVENTURES

TOP 10 DAY TRIPS & EXCURSIONS FROM OSLO

A day excursion from Oslo presents an excellent opportunity to explore different parts of the country, and even venture into neighboring Sweden, all without the need to pack up and spend a night in another city. For those with limited time, numerous activities await just beyond the city center. One option is to explore the picturesque Bygdoy Peninsula, renowned for its impressive museums and exceptional architecture. Another enticing option is the Ekeberg neighborhood, easily reachable via public transportation.

Reliable train, bus, and boat services make it convenient for visitors to reach various captivating destinations within a 2.5-hour radius or less, many of which are situated along Oslofjord. Along this route, one can discover a diverse range of attractions, from Viking settlements and fortresses to amusement parks and shopping areas, not to mention an array of captivating museums. Make the most of your day trips from Oslo by referring to our curated list of the finest options below:

1. BYGDOY PENINSULA

Located just four miles west of Oslo, Bygdoy Peninsula is a must-visit destination for those with an interest in Norwegian history, culture, and breathtaking natural scenery. Whether you choose to arrive by public transport or car, Bygdoy welcomes visitors with a plethora of museums, parks, beaches, and forests, making it an ideal spot for a day trip or even as a base for your stay in Oslo.

Journey into the Past: *Center for Studies of Holocaust and Religious Minorities in Norway:* Housed in the elegant Villa Grande, this center provides a deep dive into the somber history of the Holocaust and religious persecution in Norway. | *Norwegian Maritime Museum:* Immerse yourself in Norway's rich maritime legacy with exhibits featuring historic boats, Viking artifacts, and the golden age of sailing. Be sure not to overlook the "Queen of Congo" ship, where children can engage with instruments and envision life at sea.

Embrace the Outdoors: *Huk & Paradisbukta Beach:* Bask in the sunshine on the sandy shores of Huk & Paradisbukta, Bygdoy's most popular beaches. Engage in a game of volleyball, grab a snack from food vendors, or unwind beneath the shade of trees. | *Explore on Foot or by Bike:* Bygdoy's forests and parks boast numerous serene trails, perfect for exploring the peninsula on foot or by bike. Uncover hidden coves, lush green landscapes, and breathtaking views of the Oslofjord. ***Beyond the Main Attractions:*** For those seeking a deeper exploration, Bygdoy has more to offer. *Visit the Norwegian Museum of Cultural History* to marvel at the Gol Stave Church, a meticulously preserved medieval church. History enthusiasts can delve into the *Royal Manor*, a fully operational 200-acre organic farm. Additionally, art aficionados can appreciate modern art at the *Astrup Fearnley Museum of Modern Art.*

2. LILLEHAMMER

Lillehammer, a highly sought-after destination for both tourists and Oslo residents, offers a plethora of activities. Situated just a two-hour train ride from Oslo, the city's Tourist Information Office conveniently sits at the train station. The highlight of Lillehammer is Maihaugen, an open-air museum featuring period homes and exhibits. It is also home to the Norwegian Olympic Museum, commemorating the 1994 Winter Olympics hosted in the city. Teeming with cultural attractions, Lillehammer boasts the Kittilbu Museum, a Postal Museum, the Road Museum, and various historic residences, including the dwelling of Nobel laureate Sigrid Undset, a renowned female writer.

Lillehammer is also a hub for vibrant art and crafts, and the *pedestrian thoroughfare Storgata* stands out as the prime destination for acquiring unique souvenirs. Winter sports enthusiasts will find Lillehammer particularly appealing with its *five ski resorts* and a range of exciting activities, such as *sleigh rides*, *dog sledding*, and *ice fishing*. Notably, former Olympic facilities like the *Lysgårdsbakkene Ski Jump* and the *Hunderfossen Luge Track* add to the allure for those who appreciate winter sports.

3. TUSENFRYD FAMILY PARK, VINTERBRO

With over 40 attractions, numerous games, and a variety of live entertainment options, TusenFryd Family Park offers an enjoyable diversion for the entire family. The park features a wide range of experiences, from exhilarating thrill rides like the Speedmonster Coaster to family-friendly favorites such as bumper cars and log boat rides. Among the most sought-after attractions are those inspired by Norse Mythology, including Thor's Hammer—an indoor 3D adventure—and Ragnarok, an intense river-rafting ride with drops and ample splashing.

The park introduces cutting-edge technology in newer attractions, such as a Virtual Reality roller coaster with a steampunk theme and a 4D haunted house. Entertainment is further enhanced with vehicle stunt shows performed by a skilled team of Italian drivers and various events held throughout the season. Park admission also grants access to the BadeFryd water park, a particular favorite among youngsters.

Located at Høyungsletta 19, 1407 Vinterbro, you can find more information on the official site: _www.tusenfryd.no/en._

4. GAMLE FREDRIKSTAD

Situated just a little over an hour away from Oslo's central station by train, this town is beloved for its 17th-century Old Town, referred to as Gamle Fredrikstad or Gamlebyen. Secured by a total of five forts, this locale stands out as the sole Norwegian fortifications that have retained their original structure. Nestled on the edge of the Glomma estuary, the city is surrounded by an impressive network of star-shaped moats, enhancing its exceptional security.

What distinguishes Gamle Fredrikstad is the impressive commitment of its inhabitants to preserve and honor the historical significance of the city while actively utilizing the space, ensuring that the town remains lively without compromising its antique allure. Visitors can fully engage in the historical ambiance by meandering through cobblestone streets, enjoying shopping, and partaking in dining experiences. For a more in-depth understanding of the life within the fortress city, tourists can explore the Fredrikstad Museum, which showcases exhibits and demonstrations.

Apart from the Old Town, visitors also have the opportunity to explore the well-maintained 17th-century Kongsten Fort and the island-based Akerøya Fort, both meticulously restored from ruins.

5. TØNSBERG

Founded by Vikings, Tønsberg holds the distinction of being Norway's oldest city and gained prominence in 1904 as the original discovery site of the renowned Oseberg Viking ship. A faithful reproduction of the Oseberg ship is available for tours in Tønsberg's harbor, where the Oseberg Viking Inheritance Foundation is actively reconstructing the Klåstad ship, employing only the methods and tools used by Vikings during their initial construction.

Tønsberg boasts the largest ruin site in Scandinavia, Mount Slottsfjell (Castle Rock), featuring the 13th-century Castle Rock Tower and the Slottsfjel Museum (Slottsfjellsmuseet). The museum showcases a Viking ship and artifacts discovered just three kilometers away, an exhibition of whale skeletons, and several displays dedicated to medieval life.

Serving as the starting point for the Vestfold Viking Trail, a historical route highlighting Viking-age burial sites and former settlements, Tønsberg attracts both Norwegians and international tourists, especially during the summer. Færder National Park, home to the picturesque Verdens Ende (World's End), further adds to the area's appeal as a popular summer vacation destination.

6. DRØBAK

Drøbak is a mere 50-minute bus ride from Oslo, but people in the know opt for the 1.5-hour boat journey—an affordable and delightful way to traverse the Oslofjord while enjoying captivating sightseeing along the route.

Among the town's primary draws for locals are its beaches and delectable fresh seafood, while tourists flock to witness Oscarsborg, a fortress that successfully defended against German troops during WWII. *Visitors can explore the fortress grounds and the ancient castle*, housing a museum and hosting cultural events in the summer, such as artisan fairs and music festivals. *Drøbak Town Square is a must-visit for shopping enthusiasts*, featuring a summer open-air market brimming with a diverse array of goods and a Christmas Market held every December. *Families can carve out time for* _the Drøbak Aquarium_, conveniently situated next to the Tourist Information Center. Open year-round, the aquarium showcases marine life native to the Drøbak Strait, with two sizable tanks housing a variety of sea creatures like sharks, octopuses, eels, and other local fish. A touch pool is also available, providing kids with the opportunity to interact up close with starfish and other small marine life.

7. KONGSBERG

Situated approximately one hour and fifteen minutes away from Oslo, with convenient train access from the capital city, Kongsberg is internationally renowned for its advanced technology enterprise, _Kongsberg Defence & Aerospace_. However, tourists are drawn to the area for the skiing opportunities at _Kongsberg Skisenter_ and to explore the historic _King's Mines_, formerly the primary source of the kingdom's silver. Operational from 1623 to 1958, the Kongsberg Silver Mines comprise over 200 individual mines, extending several kilometers into the mountain.

Between May and the end of August, visitors have the chance to tour the mine using the rail system once utilized by workers. It's advisable to bring a sweater, as temperatures can drop to as low as 6 degrees Celsius. In close proximity, the _Norwegian Mining Museum_ houses the world's largest native silver collection, featuring exhibits on coin production and the mine's history.

8. ONSTAD ART CENTER, HØVIKODDEN

Established in 1966, the Henie-Onstad Art Center, situated in Høvikodden, hosts Norway's largest collection of international art, showcasing works by acclaimed artists like Matisse, Miró, and Picasso, alongside trophies earned by the accomplished skater Sonja Henie. The center also offers interactive art programs for children, including Labben, an open studio where both children and parents can explore their creativity under the guidance of the staff.

Beyond its rich art collection, the Art Center functions as a venue for diverse cultural events, including theatrical performances and concerts. Surrounding the center, visitors can enjoy the seamlessly integrated Sculpture Park, situated within a network of trails along the shores of the

Oslo Peninsula.

Address: Sonja Henies vei 31, 1311 Høvikodden
Official Website: www.hok.no

9. TAKE A TRAIN TO FLÅM

Embarking on a rail journey not only evokes a sense of nostalgia but also provides you with the opportunity to discover pristine, untouched landscapes. The primary leg of the trip commences from Oslo Central Station, heading southwest.

Upon reaching **Haugastøl**, passengers bid farewell to familiar civilization and traverse northwest, passing through **Hallingskarvet National Park**. Along the route, hikers and sporadic rest huts are scattered amidst alpine flora, with grazing deer enhancing the scenic panorama. Negotiating mountain tunnels, the tracks wind into the valley, eventually reaching Myrdal.

At **Myrdal**, travelers transfer to the Flåm Railway, proceeding through the northern valley towards *Flåm*—a serene town nestled at the tip of the *Aurlandsfjord*. In Flåm, the *Flåmsbana Museum* awaits adjacent to the train station, and the historic *Frenthiem Hotel*, a splendid four-star accommodation with water vistas. Despite its small size, Flåm is a charming haven, boasting local shops, a bakery, cafés, and several vantage points to enjoy fjord views.

If you desired an extended fjord adventure, cruises depart from Flåm to explore the Sognefjord, Norway's longest and deepest fjord.

10. KARLSTAD, SWEDEN

Situated along the route between Oslo and Stockholm, the city of Karlstad is well over the border into Sweden but still within the convenient reach of a day trip, approximately 2.5 hours from the city. Karlstad takes pride in its reputation as the "*sunniest place in Sweden*," making it a favored destination for locals who come to enjoy the scenic *Lake Vänern*. You can also indulge in the city's attractions, including the *Värmlands Museum*, housed in the remarkable Chinese-temple-style building called *Cyrillushuset*, showcasing an array of fine art and captivating architecture.

Another notable site in Karlstad is the ***Brigade Museum***, offering insights into daily life in Sweden from the 1940s through the 1990s. The museum exhibits a diverse collection of military and civilian artifacts related to WWII and the Cold War. You can also engage with an ***interactive target practice simulator***, providing a firsthand experience of firing from a tank and rifle.

DAY TRIPS BY CAR: ART, CRAFTS AND INDUSTRIAL HISTORY

KISTEFOS MUSEUM AND SCULPTURE PARK

Explore the renowned Kistefos Museum and Sculpture Park, situated just an hour's drive from Oslo in Jevnaker. This world-class art museum features a diverse collection of modern and contemporary art, showcasing works by notable artists like Edvard Munch, Auguste Rodin, and Jeff Koons. The adjacent sculpture park, nestled in a picturesque natural setting, showcases creations by some of the globe's leading sculptors.

HADELAND GLASSVERK

Discover the historical charm of Hadeland Glassverk, located in Jevnaker, an hour's drive from Oslo. Operating since 1762, this venerable glassworks stands as one of Norway's oldest. You can delve into the rich history of glassmaking, observe skilled glassblowers in action, and acquire exquisite glassware directly from the factory.

BLAAFARVEVÆRKET

Embark on a journey to Blaafarveværket, a former mining and pigment factory situated in Modum, approximately 90 minutes from Oslo. Established in 1772, this facility was once the world's largest indigo producer. Now transformed into a museum and cultural center, Blaafarveværket offers a range of activities, from guided tours to exhibitions and concerts.

BÆRUMS VERK

Experience the historical ambiance of Bærums Verk, an industrial town founded in the 17th century, just 20 minutes from Oslo in Bærum. Once a major iron production hub, it has evolved into a popular tourist destination featuring shops, restaurants, and museums.

FETSUND LENSER – LUMBER MUSEUM

Journey to Fetsund lenser, a historic lumber museum located in Fetsund, roughly 45 minutes from Oslo. This museum recounts the tale of Norway's lumber industry through captivating exhibits, including a working sawmill, a boathouse, and a timber yard.

Select the perfect day trip based on your interests. For art enthusiasts, Kistefos or Blaafarveværket are ideal choices. History and culture buffs may find Hadeland Glassverk or Bærums Verk appealing, while those intrigued by the lumber industry will enjoy exploring Fetsund lenser.

GREEN DAY TRIPS IN THE OSLO REGION WITH BUS AND TRAINS

Oslo's surrounding area offers a wealth of charming destinations perfect for eco-conscious day trips via public transport. Here's a breakdown of your proposed itinerary:

1. EIDSVOLL: DIVE INTO NORWEGIAN HISTORY (TRAIN)

Eidsvoll's claim to fame lies in the grand **_Eidsvollbygningen_**, where Norway's Constitution was inked in 1814. This neoclassical mansion, now a museum, resonates with the echoes of a nation's birth.

Beyond the halls of history, Eidsvoll unfolds its verdant beauty. The glistening **_Vorma River_** snakes through the landscape, inviting leisurely strolls or invigorating kayak paddles. Lush forests cloak rolling hills, offering scenic hiking trails and tranquil picnic spots. The village itself exudes a timeless charm. Pastel-hued houses line cobbled streets, while local shops and cafes tempt with traditional wares and warm smiles. Immerse yourself in the gentle rhythm of rural life, a welcome respite from the city's bustle.

Green Travel: Take the train directly from Oslo Central Station to Eidsvoll Verk stasjon (1 hour). Explore the village and Bjørkelangen by bike (rentals available) or enjoy scenic walks along the river.

Pro Tip: Combine your historical visit with a picnic lunch amidst the picturesque landscape.

2. ÅSGÅRDSTRAND: "WHITE PEARL" OF OSLO FJORD (BUS)

Quaint, colorful houses line the waterfront, casting playful reflections in the calm waters. Boats bob gently, adding to the idyllic scene. Pristine sands beckon for sunbathing and leisurely strolls. Breathe in the crisp sea air and let the rhythmic waves lull you into serenity. | Åsgårdstrand has long captivated artists, including the iconic Edvard Munch. Explore galleries brimming with local talent, or visit the Munch Hus for a dose of artistic inspiration. During the warmer months, cafes spill onto cobbled streets and the harbor buzzes with life. Savor fresh seafood and soak up the carefree atmosphere.

Green Travel: Take bus 150 from Oslo Bussterminal to Åsgårdstrand (1.5 hours). Explore the town on foot, soaking in the coastal atmosphere. Rent a kayak or paddleboard for a closer look at the fjord.

Pro Tip: Visit the picturesque Åsgårdstrand Church and climb the hill for panoramic views. Savor fresh seafood at the harbor's cafes.

3. KISTEFOS: AN ARTISTIC ODYSSEY (COMBINED BUS & TRAIN)

Modern sculptures dance amidst a vibrant sculpture park, kissed by the gushing Randselva River. Renowned museum and industrial heritage stand in harmony, echoing with creativity. ⬛ A sensory feast for art lovers and nature enthusiasts alike.

Green Travel: Take bus 100 from Oslo Bussterminal to Jessheim stasjon (30 mins). Then, catch the train to Jevnaker stasjon (20 mins), followed by a short taxi ride to Kistefos (or a scenic 45-minute walk).

Pro Tip: Combine your museum visit with a stroll through the sculpture park, enjoying the art and nature fusion. Pack a picnic lunch to relish under the open sky.

A DAY TRIP BY THE WATERS

VERDENS ENDE

Escape the vibrant streets of Oslo and embark on an awe-inspiring day excursion to Verdens Ende, also known as "The World's End," situated within Færder National Park. This striking promontory on the southern tip of Tjøme island presents breathtaking coastal vistas, rugged rock formations, and a sensation of standing on the brink of the world.

Your Journey Unfolds: Start your day early with a picturesque train journey from Oslo Central Station to Tønsberg, Norway's oldest town. From there, take a bus or taxi to Verdens Ende, approximately a 30-minute ride. Traverse through charming villages & verdant farmlands, building anticipation for the dramatic coastline ahead.

Arriving at the World's End: Upon reaching Verdens Ende, inhale the salty air while beholding the expansive Skagerrak strait. Explore the meandering walking paths along the rocky shore, providing captivating panoramas of the archipelago and the distant horizon. Feel the ocean spray on your face as you stand on the weathered rocks, smoothed by centuries of ocean currents.

The Iconic Leaning Lighthouse: Do not overlook the iconic leaning lighthouse, a symbol of Verdens Ende since 1932. Its tilted mast, a consequence of shifting bedrock, adds to the allure of the location. Envision the tales it might recount of shipwrecks, storms, and generations of sailors guided by its flickering light.

A Seafood Enthusiast's Paradise: Indulge in a delectable seafood lunch at one of the charming restaurants overlooking the harbor. Relish fresh fish and shellfish directly from the Skagerrak, accompanied by crisp salads and locally-baked bread. The taste of the sea will linger on your palate long after your departure.

Exploring Færder National Park: Verdens Ende serves as the gateway to Færder National Park, a haven of natural beauty. Hike through coastal forests bustling with birdlife, kayak through sheltered coves, or simply unwind on a secluded beach, basking in the warm summer sun. Keep an eye out for seals on the rocks or dolphins frolicking in the waves.

A Unforgettable Return: As the day concludes, witness the sun painting the

sky with vibrant hues of orange and pink before bidding adieu to Verdens
Ende. Take the ferry back to Tønsberg, where you can stroll through quaint
streets and admire colorful wooden houses. Then, board the train back to
Oslo, carrying memories of a day spent at the edge of the world, eternally
etched in your mind.

GETTING TO VERDENS ENDE

Bus: Take Vy Buss route 150/151 from Oslo bussterminal for a
straightforward journey lasting 1 hour 45 minutes to 2 hours. Buses operate
every 30-60 minutes, with ticket prices ranging from 230-350 NOK. | **Train
and Bus:** Opt for a slightly faster and scenic route by taking a train from Oslo
Central Station to Tønsberg, followed by a bus to Verdens Ende. The train
journey lasts around 1 hour, and the bus journey from Tønsberg to Verdens
Ende takes an additional 30-45 minutes. Costs are approximately 170-260
NOK for the train and 50-80 NOK for the bus. | **Car:** If you prefer flexibility,
drive to Verdens Ende via E18 and Fv308, taking about 1 hour 20 minutes for
the 87 km journey. Note that parking at Verdens Ende may be limited during
peak seasons and weekends. | **Ferry in Summer:** During June to August, enjoy
a scenic ferry ride from Aker Brygge in Oslo to Verdens Ende lasting around 2
hours 30 minutes.

EMBARK ON AN ENDURING VOYAGE ABOARD THE SKIBLADNER

Envision yourself gliding over the serene surface of Norway's largest lake,
Lake Mjøsa, on the Skibladner, a majestic paddle steamer that has graced
these waters for over 160 years. Recognizable by its elegant white hull &
iconic red paddle wheels, the Skibladner offers a nostalgic journey back in
time, a romantic experience of classic travel.

Boarding the SKiblander: To reach the Skiblander from Oslo, you need to
get to a town called Gjøvik, the main boarding point. Consider taking a direct
train from Oslo Central Station to Gjøvik, a 1-hour and 15-minute scenic ride.
Check schedules and purchase tickets on the Norges Statsbaner (NSB) website
(*https://www.vy.no/en*). From the Gjøvik train station, it's a pleasant 15-
minute walk to the pier or a quick taxi ride. | Alternatively, you can opt for a
bus from Oslo Bus Terminal to Gjøvik, taking around 1 hour and 30 minutes.
Check schedules and buy tickets on Nettbuss (*https://www.redbus.com/bus-
travels/nettbuss*). Once at the Gjøvik bus terminal, a 20-minute walk or a short

taxi ride will bring you to the pier.

Embark on a delightful day aboard the Skibladner, where the welcoming aroma of coffee and pastries sets the tone. Enjoy the unhurried pace, savoring lush forests, charming villages, and majestic mountains as the ship sails through scenic landscapes. Keep an eye out for playful otters and graceful swans accompanying the journey.

Delve into Skibladner's rich history as an onboard guide narrates tales, highlighting its role as a transportation link and its evolution into a beloved tourist attraction. Discover the diverse array of distinguished passengers, from royalty to artists. Midway through the journey, relish a delectable lunch in the refined restaurant with locally sourced ingredients and traditional preparation. Enjoy panoramic views, lively conversations, and a warm atmosphere that immerses you in a timeless tradition.

After lunch, the Skibladner journey offers the option to disembark at charming lakeside towns for leisurely exploration. Visit historic sites like Eidsvollbygningen, where the Norwegian constitution was signed, or wander through Hamar, home to the Vikingskipet Olympic arena, gaining unique insights into Norwegian culture and history. The afternoon concludes as the sun sets, casting a vibrant sky as you return to the ship. Enjoy a sense of tranquility on deck with a warm beverage, surrounded by breathtaking landscapes. As the Skibladner navigates back to Gjøvik, you'll carry lasting memories of a day immersed in history, transcending a mere trip to become a memorable encounter.

Tips for Your Skibladner Day Trip:

Tickets: Ensure to book your tickets in advance, especially during peak seasons. | *Departure Days:* The Skibladner primarily operates on Wednesdays and Saturdays during the season. | *Routes and Times*: There are several routes offered, each with different departure times. For example, the popular round trip from Gjøvik to Lillehammer takes approximately 5 hours. | *Checking the Schedule:* The best way to get the most up-to-date information about the schedule is to check the Skibladner website *https://www.skibladner.no/home* closer to your planned travel date. You can find the specific departure times for each route and day there. <u>NOTE:</u> Scheduled sailings available for the public will commence in June 2024.

CHAPTER 8: OSLO ON A BUDGET

Maximize your time in Oslo without overspending! The fjord-side green city offers abundant attractions for budget-conscious travelers. Creating lasting memories in Oslo on a budget is entirely feasible with numerous free-entry attractions, an abundance of street art, outdoor sculptures, and architectural marvels. A stroll along the harbor promenade, extending from the renowned Opera House to the Astrup Fearnley Museum, comes highly recommended. For those seeking nature, easily accessible and affordable hikes are available just a short subway ride away. Staying downtown offers you a chance to swim in the fjord, enjoy Oslo's parks, go on a budget-friendly city bike adventure and explore affordable eateries nearby. Below are budget-friendly ideas for your Oslo visit, ensuring a memorable Oslo experience without breaking the bank.

BUDGETING ADVICE

Navigating the vibrant city of Oslo on a budget is key to maximizing your experience. Let's design an affordable plan that ensures you make the most of Oslo:

LODGING: Hostels and Guesthouses: Oslo boasts a lively hostel scene. Explore options like Anker Hostel, Haraldsheim Youth Hostel, or the centrally situated CityBox Oslo, offering dorm beds starting at approximately 200 NOK per night for a social atmosphere. | **Apartments:** Airbnb presents comfortable & cost-effective apartment choices, often equipped with kitchens, enabling savings on meals. Look into areas like Grünerløkka or Majorstuen for good value. **Camping**: Experience urban camping at Camp Bjørvika, adjacent to the Opera House, at around 250 NOK per night. Picture waking up to breathtaking fjord panoramas!

DINING EXPERIENCES: **Street Food:** Oslo's dynamic street food scene offers delectable and budget-friendly options. Explore Vippa or Oslo Street Food in Torggata for trendy selections or grab a classic "pølse" (hot dog) from a street vendor. | **Lunch Buffets:** Numerous restaurants offer reasonably priced lunch buffets, ideal for sampling local delicacies such as fish stew or "brunost" (brown cheese), typically priced around 100-150 NOK. | **Picnics:** Leverage Oslo's parks and waterfront areas. Procure fresh groceries from a supermarket or bakery and relish a budget-friendly picnic. Bygdøy island offers striking vistas for an economical outdoor feast.

GETTING AROUND: *Walking and Cycling:* Embrace exploring Oslo on foot or by bike for a cost-free, healthy experience that allows you to soak in the city's allure. Rent a bike for approximately 100 NOK (10 usd) per day or join a complimentary walking tour for insider perspectives. | *Public Transport:* Oslo's efficient public transport system is both affordable and convenient. Consider purchasing a day pass around 120 NOK (12 usd) for unrestricted travel within the city center. | *Ferry Excursions:* Opt for a ferry ride across the fjord to relish spectacular views and access islands like Bygdøy with its museums. Fares are reasonable, presenting a scenic and budget-friendly adventure.

UNCOVERING HIDDEN GEMS: **Free Museums:** Several museums offer complimentary entry on specific days. Visit the National Gallery on Thursdays or the Munch Museum on Sundays for an art-filled experience without spending a penny. | **Outdoor Pursuits:** Take a dip in the fjord at Havfruenparken or partake in a free yoga session in one of the city's numerous parks—an immersion in nature and well-being without cost. | **Local Events:** Explore cost-free or reasonably priced local events such as concerts, markets, and festivals. Consult Oslo's event calendar for hidden gems aligned with your interests.

EXTRA POINTERS: **Bring a reusable water bottle:** Oslo's tap water is drinkable, saving on expenses for bottled water. | **Prepare meals at your accommodation:** Access to kitchen facilities can significantly reduce dining costs. | **Consider an Oslo Pass:** If planning to visit multiple museums and attractions, this pass could offer substantial savings. | **Embrace the off-season:** Prices for flights and accommodations tend to be lower outside peak times, stretching your budget further.

FREE ATTRACTIONS IN OSLO

1. 22 July Centre: Documenting 2011 terror attacks in Oslo & Utøya island. | **2. Aamot Bridge:** An inscription-bearing bridge transported to Oslo in 1957, crossing the Akerselva river. | **3. Akershus Fortress:** Uncover Oslo's history in the heart of the city. | **4. Akrobaten Pedestrian Bridge:** A 206-meter-long bridge stretching across Oslo central station tracks. | **5. Bjørvika Barcode:** Twelve narrow high-rise buildings in Bjørvika with distinctive architecture. | **6. Botanical Garden:** A vast garden at Tøyen | **7. Church Ruins in Maridalen**: Ruins of the Margareta Church | **8. Damstredet & Telthusbakken:** A charming part of central Oslo with well-preserved wooden houses. | **9. Deichman Bjørvika / Oslo Public Library, Main Branch:** Oslo's main library offering literature, art, films, and lectures. | **10. Ekebergparken Sculpture Park:** Blending nature, history, and art. | **11. Ibsen Sitat:** Art with 69 stainless steel quotes from Henrik Ibsen. | **12. Monastery Ruins at Hovedøya**: Middle Ages monastery ruins on the island of Hovedøya.

13. Oslo Cathedral: Originally consecrated in 1697. | **14. Oslo City Hall:** Inaugurated in 1950. | **15. Peer Gynt Sculpture Park:** Sculptures inspired by Henrik Ibsen's play "Peer Gynt." | **16. Stolpersteine:** Memorial Cobblestones: World War II memorials. | **17. The Norwegian Cancer Society's Science Centre | 18. The Norwegian National Opera & Ballet:** An iconic building housing the Norwegian National Ballet and Opera. | **19. The Ruins of St. Mary's Church**: Medieval church ruins dating back to 1050 AD. | **20. The Salmon – Science Centre:** A restaurant and educational institution focusing on Norwegian salmon. | **21. The Stovner Tower:** A footpath among the treetops at Stovner. | **22. Tjuvholmen**: Where fjord views meet contemporary architecture. | **23. Vigeland Sculpture Park:** Sculptures by Gustav Vigeland inside Frogner Park. | **24. Vulkan:** A sustainable neighborhood in the heart of Oslo.

LESS THAN $20 DINING VENUES IN OSLO

Discover places where you can enjoy dinner for less than 200 NOK with the following suggestions. Please note that the cost of beverages is not considered, and alcoholic drinks tend to be pricier in Norway due to excise taxes. We recommend accompanying your meal with free and delicious tap water. While there are many reasonably priced restaurants beyond our list, Grønlandsleiret and Torggata streets are particularly recommended for affordable dining. Additionally, most parts of the city offer numerous take-away choices, including kebabs and burgers. Explore the following budget-friendly dining options:

1. Oslo Street Food: A lively food hall in the city center with a DJ on Fridays and Saturdays. | **2. Kaffistova**: A cafeteria featuring traditional Norwegian food and cakes. | **3. Restaurant Schrøder:** A classic pub and restaurant at St. Hanshaugen offering traditional Norwegian food in a relaxed atmosphere. | **4. Café Sara**: A cozy bar and restaurant in central Oslo with an extensive selection of beer and food, along with a spacious backyard. | **5. Freddy Fuego Burrito Bar**: Offers freshly made burritos with a choice of fillings, all prepared without freezing or frying. | **6. Thai City Grüner:** A simple restaurant next to the Akerselva river offering good, affordable Thai food. | **7. Vippa Oslo:** A vibrant food court with flavors from around the world. | **8. El Camino**: A Mexican restaurant at Frogner. | **9. Ricksha Pakistani Street Food**: Started as a food truck, now offering tasty Pakistani food at festivals. | **10. Istanbul Restaurant:** Serves Turkish cuisine in a family-friendly atmosphere with fresh, authentic ingredients. | **11. Syverkiosken**: One of the last hotdog kiosks in Oslo, offering sausages prepared in the traditional way. | **12. Nam Fah**: A place serving authentic Thai cuisine with various curries and fresh ingredients. | **13. Dovrehallen Bar & Restaurant:** An informal place with a friendly atmosphere, offering traditional homemade Norwegian food at affordable prices. | **14. Tullins Café:** A casual café and bar by Holbergs plass with a relaxed atmosphere and reasonable prices. | **15. Rice Bowl Thai Café**: An informal restaurant near Karl Johan street with a diverse menu of Thai dishes. | **16. Tuk Tuk Thai**: A Thai restaurant in central Oslo decorated with bamboo from Thailand, offering a large menu with wok dishes, noodle dishes, and curries. | *17. Postkontoret:* A bar and restaurant at Tøyen serving excellent Italian-style pizza until 11 pm. | *18. Haralds Vaffel*: A waffle shop specializing in crispy chicken wings, legs, and breasts with proper sides. | *19. Fly Chicken Steen & Strøm*: Specialized in fried chicken, serving crispy chicken wings, legs, and breasts with loaded sides. | *20. Krishnas Cuisine*: Vegetarian restaurant at Majorstua with vegan and gluten-free dishes, offering take-away and catering. | *21. MelaCafé:* A café and restaurant inspired by Palestinian, Lebanese, Turkish, and Syrian culinary traditions. | *22. Dattera til Hagen:* A colorful bar and café with a charming backyard. | *23. Mamma Pizza Osteria:* A casual eatery serving authentic Italian pizza made with fresh, seasonal ingredients and imported hams and cheeses from Italy. | *24. Mediterranean Grill:* A street food restaurant in Torggata street, a popular nightlife area, where you can order shish, shawarma, and more.

AFFORDABLE PLACES TO STAY IN OSLO

In Oslo, accommodation costs can affect your travel budget, but economical options exist. Basic lodging is cheaper, and if you have a tent, you can pitch it for free in the forest or on Langøyene Island. Hostels and campsites provide affordable options with water and electricity. For comfort on a budget, explore pensions, guest houses, or budget-friendly hotels near the city center. Check out our list of budget-friendly accommodations below:

1. Citybox Oslo: An economy hotel in the city center. | *2. Anker Hotel:* Enjoy a cheap, central, and urban stay with comfort at Anker Hotel, providing a convenient base for your Oslo adventures. | *3. Cochs Pension:* A centrally located pension offering reasonable prices. | *4. Topcamp Bogstad Camping*: A year-round camping site next to the Nordmarka woods. | *5. Thon Hotel Spectrum:* A hotel close to Oslo Spectrum event arena and the central station. | *6. Oslo Youth Hostel Haraldsheim*: A youth hostel located 4 km from the city center. | *7. Thon Hotel Munch*: A hotel with a quiet yet central location. | *8. Thon Hotel Astoria:* A budget hotel in the city center. | *9. Anker Apartment - Grünerløkka*: Accommodation focusing on practicality, ease, and comfort. Offers one-room apartments. | *10. Topcamp Ekeberg Oslo:* Stay in relaxing, green surroundings with easy access to the city center. | *11. Lovisenberg Guest House:* Accommodation in quiet surroundings in central Oslo with a diaconal history dating back to 1868. | **12. Sta. Katarinahjemmet:** A guest house centrally located in a quiet part of Majorstua, run by a Catholic congregation of Dominican Sisters.

BUDGET-FRIENDLY SIGHTSEEING OPTIONS IN OSLO

Become your own tour guide with our suggestions for authentic and low-budget sightseeing. Embarking on your own exploration is not only exciting but also educational. Just remember to put on comfortable shoes for your adventures!

1. Island Hopping in the Oslo Fjord: Take a ferry and explore the islands in the inner Oslo Fjord for a unique experience.

2. Bicycle Route: Around Bygdøy: Enjoy a delightful and romantic bicycle tour around Bygdøy, featuring lush woods and park-like countryside.

3. Bicycle Route: The Vantage Point Ekeberg: Cycle to several vantage points within reach of the city center, offering scenic views.

4. Sightseeing Tour with Tram 12: Take a tram ride on line 12 to independently explore popular attractions in Oslo.

5. Free Tour Oslo: Join guided walking tours in English with community tourist guides showcasing main sights in the city center.

6. Oslo Escape Routes: Design: Follow a suggested walk between two exciting neighborhoods, exploring top design destinations.

7. Oslo Escape Routes: Architecture: Take a walk through Oslo's newest architectural wonders with this suggested route.

8. Oslo Escape Routes: Art: Explore central Oslo with a walking route designed for art lovers, featuring nine interesting stops.

9. Sightseeing Tour with Tram 19: Travel from Majorstuen on the west side to Ljan in southeastern Oslo with tram number 19.

Enjoy budget-friendly sightseeing and make the most of your time in Oslo with these do-it-yourself explorations.

EXPLORE OSLO'S ART SCENE ON A BUDGET

Experience art in various forms without breaking the bank. Oslo's growing gallery scene offers numerous free showrooms, allowing you to immerse yourself in art without spending a dime. From photography to intriguing installations, these galleries provide a diverse cultural experience.

1. Fotografiens Hus - Photo Gallery: Central Oslo gallery dedicated to photography.

2. Galleri Haaken: Established in 1961, showcasing significant Norwegian and international artists.

3. Galleri Heer: Contemporary art gallery presenting a broad spectrum of artists.

4. Fotogalleriet - Photo Gallery: Oslo's only gallery devoted to camera-based art, operating since 1977.

5. Tegnerforbundet - The Norwegian Drawing Center: Gallery with a dedicated sales department showcasing the art of drawing.

6. Galleri K: Features trendy Norwegian & international artists.

7. Blomqvist Auction House Gallery: Norway's largest art shop and auction house, established in 1870.

*8. Galleri Norske Grafikere:*** Contemporary print gallery with art by Norwegian and international artists.

9. Kunstnerforbundet: Gallery and workshop run by artists.

10. Galleri LNM: Run by The Association of Norwegian Painters, producing about 11 exhibitions per year.

11. RAM Galleri: Leading exhibition space for modern handicrafts and art with changing exhibitions.

12. Soft Galleri: Exhibits the work of Norwegian Textile Artists' members. | *13. Kunsthall Oslo:* Non-profit art space in Bjørvika presenting international contemporary art. | *14. Peder Lund:* Gallery at Tjuvholmen featuring international modern and contemporary art. | *15. Fineart Oslo:* Norway's largest gallery with a diverse collection of prints, photographs, paintings, and more. | *16. Galleri Brandstrup:* Modern gallery focusing on Nordic trendy art. | *17. Galleri Schaeffers Gate 5:* Independent art, music, and performance exhibition space. | *18. Pushwagner Gallery:* Located at Tjuvholmen, showcasing the work of one of Norway's important contemporary artists. | **_19. Galleri TM51:_** Contemporary art gallery featuring a combination of young and established artists. | **_20. Galleri Semmingsen:_** Art gallery at Frogner exhibiting paintings, photography, prints, sculptures, and installations. | **_21. Kunstplass Contemporary Art [Oslo]:_** Exhibition space for contemporary art with limited opening hours. | **_22. Galleri Mini:_** Gallery in Gamlebyen mainly exhibiting art by young artists. | **_23. Standard (Oslo):_** Gallery promoting contemporary Norwegian artists internationally. | **_24. Oslo Galleri:_** Located in the Vika borough, showing works by new and established artists. | **_25. Galleri Briskeby:_** Features a broad selection of art prints by Norwegian artists. | **_26. Shoot Gallery:_** Norway's oldest privately owned gallery for fine art photography. | **_27. Grafill:_** R21, the gallery and exhibition room of Grafill, hosts temporary exhibitions. | **_28. Buer Gallery:_** Established in 2020, a gallery for Norwegian and international contemporary art.

Delve into the diverse and accessible art offerings that Oslo has to offer without spending a penny.

EXPLORE FREE PARKS & OUTDOOR ATTRACTIONS

No matter the season – winter, summer, spring, or fall – spending a day outdoors is a unique experience! Oslo boasts abundant green spaces, from parks to forested areas. Surprisingly, the geographical center of Oslo lies within the forest between Sognsvann and Maridalsvannet lakes. However, nature isn't confined to the woods; the city's numerous parks provide excellent opportunities for relaxation. In warmer months, these parks become the preferred meeting spots for locals, and the bright summer nights make leaving difficult. These parks offer ideal settings for quality family time. Whether you're interested in admiring sculptures, playing in playgrounds, or organizing a picnic with activities like football or badminton, the parks cater to diverse preferences. So, grab a cup of coffee, put on some comfortable shoes, and enjoy these naturally green attractions: for free.

1. Sognsvann Lake: A recreation area with opportunities for picnics, swimming, fishing, walking, running, & cross-country skiing.

2. Hovedøya Island: The island closest to the city center, featuring beautiful forests, beaches, and cultural heritage.

3. Frysja / Brekkedammen: A recreation area by Maridalsvannet lake, situated at the northern end of the Akerselva river, with a waterfall and the Norwegian Museum of.

4. Torshovdalen: A park offering a great view of Oslo and the Oslo fjord, located between the boroughs of Torshov and Sinsen.

5. Akerselva River: Running through the center of Oslo, a popular recreation area with parks and walking trails.

6. Botanical Garden: A large garden at Tøyen with a diverse range of botanical specimens and an Arboretum.

7. St. Hanshaugen: One of Oslo's largest parks, north of the city center, offering recreational opportunities.

8. Langøyene Island: Accessible by ferry, featuring a big beach, a shop, a nudist beach, and a beach volleyball court.

9. Huk & Paradisbukta Beach: Beautiful beaches at Bygdøy.

10. Bygdøy: Museums, beaches, and nature trails just outside the city center.

11. Waterfall at Mølla: The most spectacular waterfall along the Akerselva river, located next to Hønse-Lovisas hus.

12. Aamot Bridge: A bridge crossing the Akerselva river with historical significance.

13. Vigeland Sculpture Park: A sculpture park inside the Frogner Park by Gustav Vigeland.

14. Birkelunden: A popular park in Grünerløkka with historical significance.

15. Sofienberg Park: The biggest park in Grünerløkka, a favorite recreational area for locals.

16. Ekebergparken Sculpture Park: A park combining nature, history, and art.

17. The Palace Park: Surrounding the Royal Palace, a popular recreational area with majestic trees.

18. The Stovner Tower: A footpath among the treetops at Stovner.

19. Tøyenparken: A large park on a hill in the middle of the Tøyenborough with expansive lawns and city views.

EXPLORE FREE EVENTS IN OSLO

Discover a variety of free events in Oslo every week, including markets, guided tours, club nights, and concerts. During the summer season, Oslo comes alive with numerous free outdoor events, including:

1. Granittrock Festival (May): Enjoy a music festival featuring various artists.
2. Musikkfest Oslo (June): Immerse yourself in the city's music festival with numerous performances.
3. VG-lista Topp 20 (June): Experience Norway's top 20 music chart event.
4. Melafestivalen (August): Join the multicultural festival celebrating diversity.

On special occasions like "**Turist i egen by**" (Be a Tourist in your own City), held every spring, and "**Kulturnatt**" (Culture Night) in autumn, numerous attractions and cultural events open their doors to the public free of charge. Don't miss the opportunity to explore Oslo without spending a penny!

Use this link: *https://www.visitoslo.com/en/whats-on/exhibitions*
to take a glance at Oslo exhibition calendar; you'll find plentiful of events that offer free entrance throughout the year . Choose the ones that appeal most to you and visit Oslo around the time of the events.

OSLO PASS

The Oslo Pass serves as an all-in-one sightseeing card, providing free entry to over 60 museums and attractions, complimentary public transportation within the city limits, and discounts on a range of activities and services in Oslo. It streamlines the visitor experience, offering both savings and efficiency during your stay in the Norwegian capital.

KEY BENEFITS OF THE OSLO PASS

Free Entry to Top Attractions: Skip the lines and enjoy complimentary access to renowned museums such as the Viking Ship Museum, the Astrup Fearnley Museum of Modern Art, and the Munch Museum. | Explore historical landmarks like Akershus Fortress and the Oslo Cathedral. | Visit family-friendly destinations like the Oslo Reptile Park and the Norwegian Museum of Science and Technology.

Free Public Transportation: Travel on trams, buses, and ferries within the city center at no cost, saving on transportation expenses. | Conveniently reach popular attractions and discover diverse neighborhoods at your own pace.

Discounts on Activities and Services: Receive discounts on various activities, including fjord cruises, bike rentals, and theater tickets. | Enjoy savings on dining at selected restaurants and cafes. | Take advantage of special offers at shops and souvenir stores.

Convenience and Time-Saving: Eliminate the need to purchase individual tickets for each attraction, streamlining the experience. | Save time with complimentary access to public transportation. | Plan your itinerary effortlessly using the Oslo Pass guidebook and map provided. **LEARN MORE:** *https://www.visitoslo.com/en/activities-and-attractions/oslo-pass*. The Oslo Pass App is available on the Apple store and Google Play store for download.

CHAPTER 9: ESSENTIAL INFORMATION & TIPS

COMMUNICATION TIPS

Language: ***1. Acquaint yourself with basic phrases:*** Even though many Norwegians are proficient in English, showing respect by knowing essential phrases like "Takk" (Thank you) and "Hei" (Hi) can make a positive impression. | ***2. Speak English without hesitation:*** Oslo locals are accustomed to tourists and are generally willing to communicate in English. | ***3. Utilize translation apps:*** Consider using apps like Google Translate for quick translations, especially when dealing with menus or signs.

Cultural Cues: ***4. Respect personal space:*** Norwegians appreciate a more reserved approach to personal space. Maintain a comfortable distance during conversations. | ***5. Be mindful of volume***: Keep noise levels in check, especially indoors and in public spaces. | ***6. Observe queuing etiquette:*** Norwegians value orderly queues. Always wait your turn, even if the line appears slow. | ***7. Opt for casual attire:*** Oslo has a laid-back atmosphere, making jeans and sneakers suitable for most occasions.

Mobile & Internet: ***8. Invest in a travel SIM card:*** Local SIM cards provide better data packages and prevent roaming charges. | ***9. Wi-Fi accessibility:*** Many restaurants, cafes, and hotels offer free Wi-Fi. | ***10. Download essential apps:*** Consider downloading apps for public transportation, maps, or language translation.

Other Tips: ***11. Wear a smile and be friendly:*** Norwegians appreciate politeness and friendly interactions. | ***12. Exercise patience***: Oslo operates at a more relaxed pace compared to bustling cities. | ***13. Embrace humor:*** Norwegians enjoy dry humor and sarcasm. A light-hearted approach can be well-received. | ***14. Seek assistance when needed:*** Most people are more than willing to help lost or confused tourists.

50 USEFUL NORWEGIAN PHRASES TO NAVIGATE YOUR WAY IN OSLO

GREETINGS & BASICS

1. Hei / Hallå - Hi / Hello | *Pronunciation:* Hay / Hal-loh

2. Ha det bra! - Goodbye! (casual) | *Pronunciation:* Ha deh bra

3. Ha det hyggelig! - Have a nice time!
Pronunciation: Ha deh hig-ge-lig

4. Takk! / Tusen takk! - Thank you! / Thank you very much!
Pronunciation: Tahk / Too-sen tahk

5. Vær så god! - You're welcome! | *Pronunciation:* Vair soh good

6. Unnskyld meg! - Excuse me! | *Pronunciation:* Unn-skyld mei

7. Ja / Nei - Yes / No | *Pronunciation:* Yah / Nay

8. Jeg forstår ikke. - I don't understand.
Pronunciation: Yei for-stor eerke

9. Kan du snakke engelsk? - Do you speak English?
Pronunciation: Kan du snak-ke eng-elsk?

10. Hyggelig å møte deg! - Nice to meet you!
Pronunciation: Hig-ge-lig o mø-te dey

GETTING AROUND

11. Hvor er...? - Where is...? | *Pronunciation:* Vor er...?

12. Kan jeg få...? - Can I get...? | *Pronunciation:* Kan yei foh...?

137

13. En billett til…, takk. - A ticket to…, please.
Pronunciation: En bil-let teel…, tahk

14. Hvor mye koster…? - How much is…?
Pronunciation: Vor moye koss-ter…?

15. Kan jeg betale med kort? - Can I pay by card?
Pronunciation: Kan yei bet-ta-le med kort?

16. Neste stopp, vær så snill. - Next stop, please.
Pronunciation: Nes-te stohp, vair soh snill

17. T-bane / Bybuss / Trikk - Metro / City Bus / Tram
Pronunciation: T-bah-ne / By-boos / Trikk

18. Flytog/Tog - Airport train/Train | *Pronunciation:* Fly-tohg / Tohg

19. Taxi, takk! - Taxi, please! *Pronunciation:* Tahk-see, tahk

20. Hvor lang tid tar det…? - How long does it take to…?
Pronunciation: Vor long teed tar deh…?

FOOD & DINING

21. Bord for, takk.. - Table for.., please. | *Pronunciation:* Bor for.., tahk

22. Kan jeg få menyen, takk? - Can I have the menu, please?
Pronunciation: Kan yei foh mei-nyen, tahk?

23. Jeg vil gjerne ha… - I would like to have…
Pronunciation: Yei vil yern-e ha…

24. Anbefaler du…? - Do you recommend…?
Pronunciation: An-be-fa-ler do…?

25. Kan jeg få regningen, takk? - Can I have the bill, please?

Pronunciation: Kan yei foh re-gen-ningen, tahk?

26. Tips er inkludert. - Tips is included.
Pronunciation: Tips er in-kloo-dert

27. God appetitt! - Enjoy your meal! | *Pronunciation:* God ap-pe-titt

28. Skål! - Cheers! | *Pronunciation:* Skohl

29. Kaffe, takk. / Te, takk. - Coffee, please. / Tea, please.
Pronunciation: Kah-fe, tahk / Teh, tahk

30. Vann, takk. - Water, please. | *Pronunciation:* Vahn, tahk

ACTIVITIES & SIGHTSEEING

31. Åpningstider, takk. - Opening hours, please.
Pronunciation: Op-ning-stee-der, tahk

32. Er det gratis inngang? - Is it free entry?
Pronunciation: Er deh gra-tis ing-gang?

33. Kan du ta et bilde av oss? - Can you take a picture of us?
Pronunciation: Kan du tah et bil-de av oss?

34. Anbefaler du noen aktiviteter? - Do you recommend any activities? |
Pronunciation: An-be-fa-ler do noen ak-ti-vi-te-ter?

35. Hva er det beste stedet å ta bilder? - Where is the best place to take
pictures? | *Pronunciation:* Va er deh be-ste sted-et å tah bil-der?

36. Jeg leter etter..., takk. - I'm looking for..., please.
Pronunciation: Yei le-ter et-ter..., tahk

37. Kan du vise meg på kartet? - Can you show me on the map?
Pronunciation: Kan du vee-se meg på kar-tet?

38. Oslofjord / Frognerparken / Akershus Festning - Oslofjord / Frogner Park / Akershus Fortress | ***Pronunciation:*** Oss-loh-fyord / Froner-park-en / A-kers-hoos Fest-ning)

39. Munchmuseet / Vikingskipmuseet / Nasjonalmuseet - Munch Museum / Viking Ship Museum / National Museum | ***Pronunciation:*** Munch-mu-se-et / Vik-ing-skip-mu-se-et / Nas-jon-al-mu-se-et)

40. Holmenkollen / Operahuset / Karl Johans gate - Holmenkollen/Opera House / Karl Johans gate | ***Pronunciation:*** Hol-men-kol-len / Oh-pe-ra-hu-set / Karl Yo-hans ga-te)

EMERGENCIES

41. Hjelp! - Help! | ***Pronunciation:*** Yelp)

42. Politi! / Brann! / Ambulanse! - Police! / Fire! / Ambulance!
Pronunciation: Poh-lee-tee / Braun / Am-bu-lanse

43. Jeg trenger legehjelp. - I need medical attention.
Pronunciation: Yeg tren-ger le-ge-yelp

44. Jeg har mistet bort meg. - I'm lost.
Pronunciation: Yeg har mis-tet bort may

45. Telefonnummeret mitt er... - My phone number is...
Pronunciation: Te-le-fon-num-mer-et meet er

BONUS

46. Tusen takk for hjelpen! - Thank you so much for your help!
Pronunciation: Too-sen tahk for yelp-en

47. Lærte du norsk på skolen? - Did you learn Norwegian in school?
Pronunciation: Lert-eh do norsk oh sko-len

48. Oslo er vakkert! - Oslo is beautiful!

Pronunciation: Oss-loh er vak-kert

49. Jeg kommer tilbake! - I'll be back!
Pronunciation: Yeg kom-mer til-bak-e

50. Ha en fortsatt god dag! - Have a great day!
Pronunciation: Ha en fort-satt good dahg

STAYING SAFE & HEALTHY

While Oslo is generally a safe city for tourists, it's prudent to be prepared. Here are some guidelines for maintaining safety and well-being during your visit:

Police: 112
Ambulance: 113
Fire: 110
General emergency number (non-emergencies): 116 117

IMPORTANT PHONE NUMBERS

Oslo Tourist Information: (+47) 23 10 62 00
US Embassy in Oslo: (+47) 21 30 85 40
UK Embassy in Oslo: (+47) 23 13 27 00
Canadian Embassy in Oslo: (+47) 22 99 53 00

HEALTHCARE INFORMATION

- Oslo tap water is safe for consumption.
- Public healthcare is accessible to all, though non-residents may encounter extended wait times. Consider carrying private health insurance for added assurance.
- Pharmacies are readily available and well-stocked.
- *Vaccinations:* Consult your doctor or travel clinic for recommended vaccinations prior to your trip.

- Having Travel insurance, particularly for medical coverage and trip cancellation protection, is highly advisable.
- Ensure your insurance covers the activities planned in Oslo, such as skiing

or hiking.

- Keep a copy of your insurance policy with you at all times.

GENERAL SAFETY TIPS

- Stay vigilant in your surroundings, especially in crowded areas.
- Secure your valuables in a safe place, like a money belt or hotel safe.
- Avoid walking alone at night, particularly in desolate areas.
- Adhere to local customs and laws.
- Steer clear of drugs and illegal activities.

ADDITIONAL RESOURCES

Norwegian Police website: *https://www.politiet.no*
Norwegian Emergency Preparedness Agency website: *https://www.dsb.no*
Norwegian Institute of Public Health website: *https://www.fhi.no* (in Norwegian, with some English information available

By adhering to these tips and staying well-informed, you can ensure a secure and healthy visit to Oslo.

ACCESSIBILITY & FAMILY TRAVEL

Oslo stands out as a city that is both family-friendly and accessible. When planning a trip with children or individuals with special needs, a bit of extra preparation can go a long way. Fear not! Here's how you can make your Oslo adventure smooth and enjoyable for everyone:

PLANNING & RESOURCES

VisitOSLO: Their website provides dedicated sections for family activities and accessibility information - *https://www.visitoslo.com/en/your-oslo/children*

Enable Oslo: Offers detailed accessibility information for various Oslo attractions. *https://xdaforums.com/t/missing-accessibility-menu-help.4178007*

Oslo Pass: Consider obtaining a pass for free public transport, discounts on attractions, and queue-skipping privileges, saving time and hassle - *https://www.visitoslo.com/en/activities-and-attractions/oslo-pass*

GENERAL ACCESSIBILITY

Public transport: Oslo boasts a well-developed network of buses, trams, metros, and ferries, many with wheelchair access and designated priority seating.

Attractions: Most museums, restaurants, and cultural venues are accessible with ramps, elevators, and adapted restrooms. Check individual websites for specifics.

Streets: Pedestrian paths are generally wide and well-maintained, with lowered curbs and crossings.

Sensory considerations: Some museums and attractions offer sensory maps or quiet hours for individuals with sensory sensitivities.

FAMILY-FRIENDLY FUN

Museums: The National Museum, Viking Ship Museum, and Nobel Peace Center offer interactive exhibits and family-friendly activities.

Outdoor Activities: Explore Frogner Park's sculptures, take a ferry ride on the Oslofjord, or visit the Holmenkollen ski jump for stunning views.

Playgrounds: Numerous vibrant playgrounds cater to all ages and abilities.

Theme Parks: TusenFryd offers thrilling roller coasters and family-friendly rides.

SPECIAL NEEDS CONSIDERATIONS

Contact individual attractions beforehand to confirm accessibility features and any specific needs you may have.

Consider accessibility aids: Pack appropriate equipment like wheelchairs, strollers, or communication tools.

Plan breaks and downtime: Factor in rest periods and adjust schedules to avoid sensory overload.

Support services: Research availability of specialized services like accessible taxis or adapted equipment rentals, if needed.

ADDITIONAL TIPS

Pack comfortable shoes and weather-appropriate clothing.

Download helpful apps like "Oslo T-bane" for public transport navigation or "RuterReise" for real-time travel updates.

Be patient and kind! Oslo residents embrace inclusivity and are happy to assist.

SUSTAINABLE TRAVEL: MAKING ECO-FRIENDLY CHOICES IN OSLO

Oslo has positioned itself as a frontrunner in sustainable tourism, providing eco-friendly alternatives for every facet of your visit. Here's how you can make conscientious decisions throughout your journey:

PUBLIC TRANSPORTATION

Walk, cycle, or take the tram: Explore the city on foot or two wheels whenever possible. Oslo is highly compact and cycle-friendly, boasting dedicated lanes and numerous rental options. The tram network is efficient and scenic, offering a charming way to traverse the city.

Purchase an Oslo Pass: This pass offers FREE travel on public transport, including ferries, saving you money & reducing emissions.

Choose trains over flights: Opt for the scenic and sustainable option of train travel for longer journeys within Norway. The extensive and comfortable rail network is an eco-conscious choice.

ECO-CONSCIOUS ACCOMMODATION

Stay in sustainable hotels: Opt for hotels with eco-friendly certifications like the Nordic Ecolabel. These establishments prioritize energy efficiency, waste reduction, and local sourcing.

Consider alternative options: Explore charming eco-lodges or guesthouses outside the city center for a more immersive experience. Hostels can also be a sustainable choice, encouraging shared spaces and reduced resource consumption.

Minimize water and energy use: Be mindful of towel usage, turn off lights when leaving rooms, and opt for shorter showers.

RESPONSIBLE ACTIVITIES

Support local businesses: Choose restaurants and shops that utilize local ingredients and products, minimizing the environmental impact of transportation.

Enjoy outdoor activities: Explore Oslo's beautiful nature reserves, go kayaking on the Oslofjord, or hike in the surrounding forests. These activities offer a healthy and sustainable way to experience the city.

Choose eco-friendly tours: Opt for tours with a focus on sustainability, such as those showcasing Oslo's green initiatives or utilizing bicycles or electric vehicles.

Minimize waste: Pack reusable water bottles and shopping bags to avoid single-use plastics. Use recycling bins appropriately and support initiatives like refill stations.

ADDITIONAL TIPS

Pack light: Bringing less luggage reduces travel emissions and makes navigating the city easier.

Offset your carbon footprint: Consider participating in carbon offsetting programs to compensate for the unavoidable emissions from your trip.

Learn about Oslo's green initiatives: Visit the Oslo Environmental Center or attend sustainability-themed events to gain a deeper understanding of the city's commitment to eco-friendliness.

By making these informed choices, you can contribute to Oslo's sustainability efforts and have a positive impact on the environment while enjoying your trip. Remember, responsible tourism benefits everyone: travelers, locals, and the planet.

SHOPPING & SOUVENIRS

Oslo's shopping landscape presents an enticing fusion of distinctive local crafts, chic designer outlets, and vintage gems. Whether your quest is for authentic Norwegian souvenirs or a desire to indulge in some retail therapy, Oslo caters to every taste and budget. Here's your handbook for navigating the city's diverse shopping districts:

UNIQUE LOCAL CRAFTS

Grünerløkka: Stroll through the quaint streets of this bohemian district, exploring independent shops such as the *Andreas Engesvik glassblowing studio* or the whimsical *Ting Oslo* for handcrafted trinkets.

Markedsgata: Experience traditional Norwegian sweaters, hand-painted ceramics, and locally-made jewelry at this historic outdoor market.

Vulkanområdet: This former industrial area hosts contemporary design studios like *TORP* and *Handwerkhuset*, showcasing the forefront of Norwegian craftsmanship.

DESIGNER DELIGHTS

Frogner: Dive into high-end fashion flagships like Louis Vuitton and Chanel for a touch of luxury.

Hegdehaugsveien: Browse trendy boutiques like Holzweiler and By Malene Birger for Scandinavian minimalism with a twist.

Tjuvholmen: This waterfront district houses sleek designer stores like Acne Studios and Filippa K alongside art galleries and cafes.

VINTAGE TREASURES

Fretexhane: Explore this treasure trove of pre-loved clothing, furniture, and household items, with locations across the city.

UFF: Another haven for vintage finds, UFF offers a diverse selection at lower price points.

Blå kiosker: Scattered throughout Oslo, these small blue kiosks sell vintage records, books, and trinkets – perfect for quirky souvenirs.

SPECIALTY SHOPPING

Bogstadveien: This avenue hosts an array of luxury homeware stores and interior design showrooms.

Mathallen Oslo: Indulge your foodie senses at this gourmet food hall, stocked with fresh produce, artisanal cheeses, and local delicacies.

Paleet Christinia: A historical department store offering everything from cosmetics and clothing to toys and homeware – a glimpse into traditional Oslo shopping.

BEYOND THE SOUVENIRS

Consider Experiences: Opt for a pottery class at Atelier Jeppe, a food tour in Grünerløkka, or a cheese-making workshop for a truly memorable souvenir.

Pack Lightly: Remember to consider baggage restrictions when buying bulky items.

Support Local: Choose independent shops and craftspeople whenever possible to contribute to Oslo's vibrant creative scene.

So, prepare to delve into and explore Oslo's unique shopping scene! From traditional crafts to contemporary designs, you're sure to unearth treasures that encapsulate the essence of this captivating city.

CHAPTER 10: THEMED ITINERARIES
3 Days Each for Different Passions

ART AFICIONADO

Morning: Commence your cultural exploration with a hearty breakfast at *Døgnvill Burger Tjuvholmen*, renowned for its gourmet burgers. | Following that, pay a visit to the majestic *Oslo Royal Palace* (Kongelige Slott) and, if scheduled, witness the Changing of the Guard. | Take a leisurely stroll through the serene Oslo Palace Park (Slottsparken) to inaugurate your day with a touch of royalty.

Afternoon: For lunch, make your way to *Fru Hagen*, a charming spot offering a diverse array of dishes. | After lunch, visit the *Norwegian Museum of Cultural History (Norsk Folkemuseum)*. Explore the open-air museum to gain insights into the country's rich heritage.

Evening: Indulge in a dining experience at the globally acclaimed *Maaemo*, a three-Michelin-starred restaurant, for an unforgettable gastronomic adventure. | Following dinner, take a tranquil evening stroll to the iconic Oslo Opera House (Operahuset). Ascend to the roof for panoramic views of the city and the fjord, a perfect way to conclude your first day in Oslo.

Morning. Initiate your day with a visit to the renowned Vigeland Sculpture Park (Vigelandsanlegget) and explore the park and its unique sculptures. | Relish a delightful breakfast at *Illegal Burger.* | Following breakfast, take a short walk to the nearby *Vigeland Museum* (Vigeland Museet) to gain a deeper understanding of the life and works of the renowned sculptor, Gustav Vigeland.

Afternoon. For lunch, indulge in authentic Italian pizzas at *Villa Paradiso Grünerløkka.* | Subsequently, take a cultural detour to the *Munch Museum* (Munchmuseet) and immerse yourself in the world of Edvard Munch, the mastermind behind the famous painting "The Scream." Explore the museum's collection of his works as well as temporary exhibitions.

Evening: Delight in a sophisticated dinner at Kontrast Restaurant, known for its innovative Nordic cuisine. As night falls, embark on a serene Oslofjord cruise, witnessing the city's stunning waterfront and surrounding islands. Opt for a cruise with audio guide commentary to learn about the history and culture of the region as you relax on the deck.

Morning: Treat yourself to a delightful breakfast at *Statholdergaarden*, offering a variety of morning delicacies. Following breakfast, explore the medieval *Akershus Castle (Akershus Slott)* and delve into its intriguing history and architecture. | From there, take a short walk to the nearby *Akershus Castle (Akershus Slott)*, where you can enjoy panoramic views of the city and the fjord.

Afternoon: For lunch, head to *Maaemo*, the three-Michelin-starred gem, for an extraordinary culinary experience. | After lunch, embark on a guided forest hike with a dog and savor traditional Norwegian waffles in the serene wilderness, a perfect way to connect with nature and the local culture.

Evening: Conclude your Oslo adventure with a sumptuous 3-course dinner cruise in the *Oslofjord*. Glide along the tranquil waters, admiring the city's skyline as you indulge in delectable dishes. The cruise offers a perfect blend of culinary delights and mesmerizing views, creating a memorable finale to your 3-day art and cuisine escapade in Oslo.

GASTRONOME EXPLORER

Morning: Begin your day with a delightful breakfast at *Fru Hagen*, celebrated for its charming atmosphere and fresh pastries. | Following that, take a leisurely stroll through the tranquil *Oslo Palace Park* (Slottsparken) and visit the grand *Royal Palace (Kongelige Slott)* to witness the changing of the guards.

Afternoon: For lunch, make your way to *Illegal Burger* and relish their inventive burger creations. After your meal, immerse yourself in the lively ambiance of *Karl Johans Gate*, Oslo's main street, exploring its boutiques and cultural landmarks. Later, visit the iconic *Oslo Opera House (Operahuset)* and appreciate the panoramic views from its rooftop.

Evening: Embark on a gastronomic adventure at *Maaemo*, a three-Michelin-starred restaurant offering a distinctive dining experience. Following dinner, take a serene *Oslofjord cruise* to admire the city's evening skyline from the water, letting the gentle breeze complement your culinary journey.

Morning: Relish a Scandinavian breakfast at *Villa Paradiso Grünerløkka*, renowned for its authentic Italian cuisine. | After breakfast, explore the world-renowned *Vigeland Sculpture Park (Vigelandsanlegget)* and be captivated by the intricate sculptures set in a picturesque park.

Afternoon: For lunch, head to *Døgnvill Burger Tjuvholmen* and savor their succulent burgers. Afterwards, delve into maritime history at the *Fram Museum (Frammuseet)* and marvel at the impressive Viking ships at the *Viking Ship Museum (Vikingskipshuset)*. Wrap up your museum tour with a visit to the *Kon-Tiki Museum* to discover *Thor Heyerdahl's* expeditions.

Evening: Dine at Statholdergaarden, a Michelin-starred restaurant offering a fusion of traditional and innovative Norwegian dishes. After dinner, embark on a guided forest hike with a dog, indulging in Norwegian waffles—a perfect way to digest and unwind in the serene natural surroundings.

Morning. Commence your day with a sumptuous breakfast at *Fru Hagen*, returning to the delightful morning ambiance. Following breakfast, embark on a _guided Oslofjord cruise_ on a silent electric boat to witness the breathtaking coastal scenery and the tranquility of the fjords.

Afternoon. Enjoy lunch at _Kontrast Restaurant_, celebrated for its innovative and visually stunning dishes. Following your meal, visit the _Norwegian Museum of Cultural History (Norsk Folkemuseum)_ on Bygdøy Peninsula to immerse yourself in Norway's rich cultural heritage.

Evening. Conclude your culinary journey with a 3-course dinner cruise in the _Oslofjord_, where you can relish beautiful views of the city's shoreline while savoring a meticulously crafted menu. The gentle sway of the boat and the evening lights will provide a perfect ambiance for your final night in Oslo.

ADVENTURE ENTHUSIAST

Morning: Kick off your day with a satisfying breakfast at _Døgnvill Burger Tjuvholmen_, celebrated for its delectable burgers. Following that, join a Best of _Oslo Walking Tour_ to acquaint yourself with the city's major attractions and hidden treasures.

Afternoon: For lunch, head to _Fru Hagen_ and revel in its lively ambiance. After your meal, explore the iconic _Vigeland Sculpture Park (Vigelandsanlegget)_ to appreciate the unique sculptures and the picturesque park surroundings.

Evening: Delight in a gastronomic adventure at _Maaemo_, a three-Michelin-starred restaurant specializing in innovative Nordic cuisine. Post-dinner, take a leisurely stroll around the _Opera House (Operahuset)_ and admire the architectural marvel illuminated at night.

Morning: Begin your day with a visit to the majestic _Holmenkollen Ski Jump_, where panoramic views of the city await. Grab a quick bite at _Illegal Burger_ before embarking on the _100% Electric Oslofjord Sightseeing Cruise_ to witness the stunning fjords.

Afternoon: Disembark and head to the _Fram Museum (Frammuseet)_ to delve into the history of polar exploration. For a late lunch, relish authentic Italian pizzas at _Villa Paradiso Grünerløkka_. Subsequently, take a guided tour of the _Norwegian Museum of Cultural History (Norsk Folkemuseum)_ to immerse yourself in Norway's cultural heritage.

Evening: Enjoy a laid-back evening at _Statholdergaarden_, known for its refined ambiance and exquisite Norwegian dishes. Conclude the night with a visit to the vibrant _Aker Brygge area_, where you can explore the waterfront and soak in the lively atmosphere.

Morning: Energize yourself with breakfast at _Kontrast Restaurant_, offering a fusion of traditional and modern Norwegian cuisine. Then, embark on a guided snowshoeing tour in the _Oslomarka Forest_, immersing yourself in the serenity of the winter landscape.

Afternoon: After working up an appetite, relish a _self-service floating sauna_ experience with a fjord view. For a late lunch, revisit _Døgnvill Burger Tjuvholmen_ to sample a different burger from their extensive menu. Spend the remainder of the afternoon at your leisure, perhaps exploring the _Bygdøy Peninsula_ and its museums.

Evening: Conclude your adventure with a 3-course dinner _cruise in the Oslofjord_, admiring the city's illuminated skyline from the water. Dine onboard while reflecting on your memorable time in Oslo.

HISTORY ENTHUSIAST

Morning: Viking Ship Museum: Witness impressive Viking ships and artifacts, learning about their seafaring adventures.

Afternoon: Akershus Fortress: Explore the medieval castle, delve into its rich history, and enjoy panoramic city views.

Evening: Oslo City Hall: Take a guided tour of this iconic landmark and learn about Oslo's political and cultural significance.

Morning: National Museum of Cultural History: Explore Norwegian history from Viking times to the present, with engaging exhibits and artifacts.

Afternoon: Holmenkollen: Visit the Holmenkollen Ski Jump, a symbol of Norwegian sporting prowess, and learn about its fascinating history.

Evening: Nobel Peace Center: Immerse yourself in the ideals of peace and human rights through interactive exhibits and historical figures.

Morning: Vigeland Mausoleum: Discover the fascinating and controversial sculptures of Emanuel Vigeland in this unique museum-mausoleum.

Afternoon: Oslo Tramway Museum: Take a nostalgic ride on a vintage tram and learn about the city's public transportation history.

Evening: Historisk Restaurant Oslo: Enjoy a traditional Norwegian meal in a historical setting, surrounded by period decor and stories.

BONUS CHAPTER

HIDDEN GEMS & OFF-THE-BEATEN-PATH ADVENTURES

Oslo's enchantment extends far beyond the renowned Viking Ship Museum and Karl Johans gate. Brace yourself to unveil concealed treasures and beloved local spots for an authentically immersive experience:

ART & CULTURE

Astrup Fearnley Museet: Nestled on the waterfront, this hidden marvel boasts a remarkable collection of modern and contemporary art, featuring works by Munch, Picasso, and Kandinsky.

Emanuel Vigeland Museum: Step into the intriguing world of sculptor Emanuel Vigeland at his mausoleum-turned-concert hall.

Intercultural Museum: Celebrate Oslo's diverse populace through temporary exhibitions and engaging events.

SALT Akershus: Explore this dynamic waterfront venue with ever-changing art installations, a floating sauna, and delectable street food.

NATURE & OUTDOOR ADVENTURES

Hovedøya Island: Board a ferry to this serene island, where medieval monastery ruins, hiking trails, and breathtaking fjord views await.

Lofossen Falls: Trek through the picturesque Lillomarka forest to discover cascading waterfalls and idyllic scenery.

Kampen Park: Uncover this hidden oasis in the city center, a peaceful haven featuring a community garden and charming picnic spots.

Vardåsen Island: Escape the urban hustle to indulge in birdwatching, swimming, and kayaking in this stunning natural reserve within city limits.

LOCAL HAUNTS & EXPERIENCES

Mathallen Oslo: Immerse yourself in this lively food hall, sampling local delicacies and engaging with passionate producers.

Vulkan Climbing Center: Ascend the walls at this trendy climbing gym offering panoramic city views, suitable for both novices and seasoned climbers.

Vippa Street Food Market: Indulge in international flavors and soak up the vibrant atmosphere at this bustling waterfront market.

Torshovparken: Join the locals for a picnic in this expansive park, hosting open-air movie screenings and community events throughout the year.

Rent a bike: Explore the city on two wheels, reaching hidden gems away from the main thoroughfares.

Join a free walking tour: Gain local insights and discover hidden gems with knowledgeable guides.

Download the Oslo Spektrum app: Stay updated on upcoming events, concerts, and exhibitions occurring during your visit.

Strike up conversations with locals: Fear not to seek recommendations from the locals; the best tips often come from unexpected sources.

Embrace the spirit of adventure and get ready to explore Oslo's hidden gems! By venturing off the beaten path, you'll encounter the city like a local, crafting enduring memories beyond the conventional tourist attractions.

SEASONAL HIGHLIGHTS

Oslo gracefully adjusts its tempo with the changing seasons, presenting a kaleidoscope of vibrant encounters throughout the year. Whether you yearn for the magic of winter, revel in the warmth of summer, or appreciate the colors of autumn, Oslo's diverse symphony of experiences is ready to be discovered. Below we compose the perfect Oslo adventure, attuned to the city's seasonal melodies!

WINTER WONDERLAND (DECEMBER - FEBRUARY)

Engage In Cross-Country Skiing: Glide through frost-covered forests at Frognerseteren, Holmenkollen, or Korketrekkeren, soaking in awe-inspiring fjord panoramas.

Indulge In Ice Skating: Twirl on the delightful rink at Spikersuppa by the Parliament Building or discover the fairytale ambiance at Vinterland in Frognerparken.

Experience Sleigh Rides: Snuggle under a blanket as a horse-drawn sleigh transports you through the wintry landscapes of Akerselva park, accompanied by the soothing clip-clop of hooves on snow.

Immerse Yourself In Christmas Markets: Revel in the festive atmosphere at Jul i Vinterland, where twinkling lights, traditional crafts, and delightful treats abound.

Explore Museums And Galleries: Find artistic solace in the Munch Museum or delve into Viking history at the Viking Ship Museum, both offering warmth and wonder.

Witness world-class performances at the iconic Oslo Opera House, a majestic glacier-inspired landmark.

SPRING AWAKENING (MARCH - MAY)

Embark on hiking and biking adventures: Traverse verdant trails in Bymarka forest or cycle along the Akerselva River, witnessing nature's vibrant resurgence.

Enjoy picnics in parks: Unfold a blanket amidst blooming flowerbeds in Frognerparken, Tøyensletta, or St. Hanshaugen, basking in the golden sunshine.

Participate in boat tours: Glide along the awakening Oslofjord, marveling at vibrant islands and charming waterfront neighborhoods.

Celebrate Norway's National Day on 17th May: Immerse yourself in the joyous festivities, featuring colorful parades, traditional costumes, and an infectious air of merriment.

Engage in concerts and events: Spring brings a vibrant calendar, from music festivals in Middelalderparken to open-air theater performances. Discover hidden gems in Oslo's museums through special exhibitions and outdoor installations.

SUMMER SYMPHONY (JUNE - AUGUST)

Embark on island hopping: Take a ferry to idyllic islands like Hovedøya or Gressholmen, where secluded beaches and hidden coves await exploration.

Take a refreshing plunge into the waters of the Oslofjord at Havfruenparken, Sørenga Sjøbad, or Tjuholmen during outdoor swimming sessions.

Organize picnics and barbecues: Gather friends and family in lush parks like Frognerparken or St. Hanshaugen for alfresco feasts and laughter.

Groove to international and local music stars at the renowned Øyafestivalen in Middelalderparken.

Celebrate inclusivity and diversity at the vibrant Oslo Pride parade and festival, an explosion of joyous color and acceptance.

Experience the magic of the midnight sun with bonfires, concerts, and celebrations throughout the city.

AUTUMNAL ENCHANTMENT (SEPTEMBER - NOVEMBER)

Continue hiking and biking adventures: Inhale the crisp air and witness the foliage ablaze with fiery hues on trails in *Korketrekkeren*, *Nordmarka forest*, or *Maridalen*.

Outdoor adventures: Engage in kayaking or canoeing on the tranquil waters of the Oslofjord, offering a serene perspective on the changing colors.

Harvest season delights: Sample the fall bounty at Akershus Fortress farmers' market or join a foraging tour in the forests to gather wild mushrooms and berries.

Seek refuge in museums and galleries: Immerse yourself in the warmth of art and history at the National Gallery or Astrup Fearnley Museum of Modern

Art.

Indulge in coffee and pastries: Relax with a steaming cup and delectable pastries at a cozy cafe, savoring the autumnal atmosphere.

Pamper yourself with a relaxing spa treatment, taking advantage of the city's abundant wellness options.

Whether your heart desires winter wonders, spring blossoms, summer sunshine, or autumnal hues, Oslo's seasonal symphony offers a melody poised to enchant you. Pack your bags, choose your season, and let the vibrant rhythm of this captivating city guide your adventure!

OSLO 2024 FESTIVAL CALENDAR

Oslo hosts a myriad of significant events, from music festivals to cultural gatherings, ensuring there's something for everyone. Delve into the vibrant cultural scene of Oslo with this overview of the major events in 2024. As a visitor planning a trip to Norway, this festival calendar will help you make the most of your time in Oslo. All you have to do is to align your visit with a special festival that suit your preference. You will see (TBC) in front of some events in 2024 which exact dates are awaiting confirmation.

JANUARY
- 18-20 Jan: Django Festival 2024 at Cosmopolite
- 25-27 Jan: Crap Comedy Festival at Parkteatret Scene

FEBRUARY
- 01 Feb: Folk dance festival at Riksscenen
- 02 Feb: Folk dance festival at Riksscenen
- 02 Feb: Nordaførr 2024 at Røverstaden
- 03 Feb: Folk dance festival at Riksscenen
- 03 Feb: Nordaførr 2024 at Røverstaden
- 09-10 Feb: Hvilepuls at Kulturkirken Jakob
- 28-29 Feb: Oslo Humorfest at SALT
- Feb. 29 - Mar 10: Holmenkollen Ski Festival

MARCH
- 01 - 02 Mar: Oslo Humorfest at SALT
- 04-08 Mar: HUMAN International Documentary Film Festival
- 07 Mar: Tjuvholmen Foodie Festival at Tjuvholmen
- 08 Mar: Oslo International Church Music Festival at Oslo (Part 1)
- March 28-31: Inferno Metal Festival

APRIL
- 10-14 Apr: Arab Film Days at Vika Kino/Oslo
- 26-28 Apr: Oslo Brass Festival at Oslo
- 27-28 Apr: Oslo Open: Open art studios at Oslo

MAY
- May 17: Norway Constitution Day Parade

- 25-26 May: Oslo Vegetarian Festival at Kubaparken
- May 30: Bislett Games | May (TBC): Oslo Medieval Festival

JUNE

- 01 Jun: National Music Day Oslo at Various Locations (Free)
- 08-09 Jun: Miniøya Children's Festival at Tøyenparken
- 13-15 Jun: Piknik i Parken Music Festival at Sofienbergparken
- 19-21 Jun: OverOslo Music Festival at Grefsenkollen
- 21-29 Jun: Oslo Pride at Oslo (Tickets on site)
- 26-29 Jun: Tons of Rock at Ekebergsletta

AUGUST

- July 27 – Aug. 3, 2024: Norway Cup
- 06-10 Aug: Øya Festival at Tøyenparken
- 11-17 Aug: Oslo Jazz Festival
- 16-18 Aug: The Mela Festival at Rådhusplassen (Free)
- Aug: Findings Festival (TBC)
- Aug: Oslo Chamber Music Festival (TBC)

SEPTEMBER

- 12-21 Sep: ULTIMA Oslo Contemporary Music Festival
- Sept. 21: Oslo Marathon
- Sept. - (TBC): By:larm | Sept. (TBC): Oslo Innovation Week

OTHERS

- Oct.-Nov. (TBC): Oslo World Music Festival
- Nov. (TBC): Film fra Sør

WHAT TO READ AND WATCH
BEFORE VISITING OSLO

Oslo presents a diverse blend of historical richness, cultural vibrancy, and natural splendor, making personalized pre-travel preparations essential for a more profound experience. Here are tailored recommendations aligned with your interests:

HISTORY AND CULTURE

BOOKS: **Sophie's World by Jostein Gaarder:** An enlightening exploration of Western thought through the eyes of a young girl, providing a charming introduction to Norwegian culture. | **Out Stealing Horses by Per Petterson:** A poignant narrative set in rural Norway, delving into themes of memory, loss, and the impact of World War II. | **One Hundred Years by Herbjorg Wassmo:** An epic saga spanning generations, offering a captivating glimpse into Norwegian social history and women's lives.

MOVIES: **Kon-Tiki (2012):** An adventurous biopic recounting Thor Heyerdahl's daring raft journey across the Pacific Ocean.
Birdemic (1967): A cult classic horror film with unintentional humor, showcasing a peculiar facet of Norwegian cinema.
Max Manus: Man of War (2008): A gripping World War II drama based on the real-life story of a Norwegian resistance fighter.

CONTEMPORARY LIFE AND THRILLS

BOOKS: **The Snowman by Jo Nesbø:** A chilling crime thriller featuring Detective Harry Hole, immersing readers in Oslo's dark underbelly. | **Love, Rosie by Cecelia Ahern:** A heartwarming and humorous novel set in Oslo, following two friends through adolescence & adulthood. | **Head Above Water by Emilie Pine:** A contemporary exploration of mental health and identity in Oslo.

FILM: **Oslo, 31 August (2011):** A poignant drama depicting a couple coping with the aftermath of a terrorist attack in Oslo. | **Hope Street (2014):** A heartwarming comedy offering a glimpse into Norwegian city life through the journey of a struggling musician. | **The King's Choice (2016):** A historical and suspenseful film exploring Norway's resistance to Nazi occupation during World War II.

LITERATURE: ***Wild by Nature:*** North Europe's Arctic Wilderness by Bernd Heinrich: A stunning natural history book showcasing the beauty and challenges of Norway's landscapes. | ***Hiking Norway's Lofoten Islands:*** A practical guide for experiencing the dramatic mountains and coastal scenery of the Lofoten Islands. | ***Winter in Oslo***: A Guide to Outdoor Activities by Lonely Planet: Explore the joys of winter in Oslo, from skiing to ice skating and frozen waterfalls.

FILM: ***The 12th Man (2017):*** An inspiring true story of survival set against the backdrop of the Norwegian mountains during World War II. | ***A Royal Affair (2012):*** A historical romance filmed partly in Oslo's Akershus Fortress. | ***Pionér (2015):*** A visually stunning adventure film about Norway's first pioneer skiers, filmed in breathtaking mountain landscapes.

These are mere suggestions! Delve deeper based on your specific interests, whether it's Viking history, contemporary art, or the Norwegian music scene. Happy exploration!

USEFUL WEBSITES

OFFICIAL AND GENERAL INFORMATION: **Explore Oslo:** The official tourism hub at *https://www.visitoslo.com/en* serves as a comprehensive resource for all aspects of Oslo travel, providing details on attractions, events, transportation, accommodation, and more. | **Oslo Municipality:** Access valuable information on public services, transport, and local news through the official city website at *https://www.oslo.kommune.no/english* | **Norway in a Nutshell:** Plan day trips and activities outside of Oslo, particularly focusing on fjords, mountains, and charming towns, by visiting *https://www.norwaynutshell.com*

TRANSPORTATION AND ACCOMMODATION: **Ruter:** Oslo's public transportation details, including bus, tram, metro, and ferry schedules and tickets, are available at *https://ruter.no/en* | **Avinor Oslo Airport:** For flight information, airport services, and transportation options to and from the airport, visit *https://avinor.no/en* | **Booking.com or Airbnb**: Explore a variety of accommodation options for all budgets in Oslo through these websites - *https://www.booking.com* or *https://www.airbnb.com*

ACTIVITIES AND ATTRACTIONS: **Oslo Highlights:** Stay informed about events, activities, and attractions occurring in Oslo during your visit by checking out the curated list at *https://www.visitoslo.com/en/whats-on*

OTHER HELPFUL RESOURCES: **Norway Today:** Stay abreast of news & events in Norway through the English-language news website at *https://www.newsinenglish.no* | **Time in Norway:** Check the current time zone & weather conditions in Oslo at *https://www.timeanddate.com/calendar/?year=2022&country=18* | **Currency Converter:** Convert your currency to Norwegian kroner using *https://www.xe.com*.

RECOMMENDED APPS

Ruter: The official app of Oslo's public transportation system is indispensable for city navigation. It furnishes real-time travel details for buses, trams, metros, and ferries, facilitating ticket purchases and journey planning.

VisitOslo: Crafted by the official tourism board, this app serves as your comprehensive Oslo guide. Access curated city guides, sightseeing recommendations, event listings, and offline maps, all in one place.

Oslo Pass: For those exploring multiple attractions, the Oslo Pass app is essential. Manage your pass, activate it, avail discounts, and plan your itinerary based on participating locations.

TRANSPORTATION AND NAVIGATION

Citymapper: This popular app offers real-time directions for walking, cycling, public transportation, and ridesharing in Oslo. Ideal for determining the quickest and most convenient routes.

Taxi2: A local taxi app that allows you to book and track your taxi in real-time, eliminating the need to hail one on the street. **Offline Maps:** Consider downloading offline maps like Google Maps or Maps.me in advance, especially if you're venturing outside the city center where data connectivity might be limited.

ACTIVITIES AND DINING

Spiseguiden: Facilitating restaurant discovery and reservations in Oslo, this app includes filters for cuisine, price range, and dietary restrictions. Read reviews and view photos before making a choice. **Eventbrite:** Uncover and secure tickets for events during your stay, ranging from concerts and theater shows to food festivals and cultural exhibitions. | VY (formerly Vy Tog): If planning day trips by train, use the VY app to purchase tickets, check schedules, and track your train in real-time.

HIDDEN GEMS AND LOCAL TIPS

Meet the Locals Oslo: Connect with locals in Oslo through this app, which facilitates guided tours, coffee meet-ups, and cultural experiences. An excellent way to explore the city through a local's perspective.

Oslo for Everyone: Offering accessibility information for individuals with disabilities, including wheelchair-friendly routes, accessible attractions, and public transportation options.

Too Good to Go: Contribute to reducing food waste and enjoy discounted meals nearing expiration at restaurants and cafes in Oslo. A win-win for your wallet and the environment.

SAY GOODBYE & TAKE A PIECE OF NORWAY WITH YOU

Oslo's cobbled streets and fjord-kissed shores recede in your rearview mirror. The vibrant energy of its museums, the delectable taste of Kjøttkaker, the echo of laughter shared with newfound friends – these memories intertwine like a vibrant tapestry, forever woven into the fabric of your being.

As you depart, a bittersweet pang may hit. But remember, Oslo hasn't left you; you've taken a piece of it with you. It's nestled in the warm glow of your camera roll, the weight of hand-knitted mittens in your bag, the lingering taste of brunost on your tongue.

Beyond the souvenirs, you carry Oslo's spirit within. The courage of the Vikings whispering in your ear, the resilience of the city's history urging you onward, the artistic spark of Munch igniting your creativity. Oslo has gifted you a new perspective, a broader lens through which to see the world. You've tasted simplicity as joy, savored nature's grandeur, and embraced the warmth of genuine human connection.

So, as you journey onwards, let Oslo's magic guide you. Share stories of its beauty, inspire others with its courage, and carry its spirit in your heart. And don't forget, the fjords are always waiting, their icy arms open to welcome you back someday.

For now, dear traveler, go forth & write your own Oslo story. May it be a tale of adventure, growth, and love for the world – a love kindled by the magic of Norway's captivating capital. Farewell, Oslo. Until we meet again.

Printed in Great Britain
by Amazon

38848960R00106